W9-CHZ-421

Preserving the
Living
Earth

ENVIRONMENT AT RISK

Preserving the
Living
Earth

CHRISTINE PETERSEN

 **Marshall Cavendish**
Benchmark
New York

Other Marshall Cavendish Offices:
Marshall Cavendish International (Asia) Private Limited, 1 New Industrial Road, Singapore 536196 • Marshall Cavendish International (Thailand) Co Ltd. 253 Asoke, 12th Flr, Sukhumvit 21 Road, Klongtoey Nua, Wattana, Bangkok 10110, Thailand • Marshall Cavendish (Malaysia) Sdn Bhd, Times Subang, Lot 46, Subang Hi-Tech Industrial Park, Batu Tiga, 40000 Shah Alam, Selangor Darul Ehsan, Malaysia

Marshall Cavendish is a trademark of Times Publishing Limited

All websites were available and accurate when this book was sent to press.

Library of Congress Cataloging-in-Publication Data

Petersen, Christine.
Preserving the living earth / Christine Petersen.
p. cm. — (Environment at risk)
Includes bibliographical references and index.
Summary: "Provides comprehensive information on Earth's various ecosystems, their importance, and the environmental threats placed upon them" — Provided by publisher.
ISBN 978-1-60870-480-4 (print) ISBN 978-1-60870-676-1 (ebook)
1. Biotic communities. 2. Environmentalism. 3. Environmental degradation. I. Title.
QH541.P445 2010
577—dc22   2010021543

Expert Reader: Dr. Amy Dunham, Assistant Professor of Ecology and Evolutionary Biology, Rice University, Houston, TX

Editor: Christine Florie
Publisher: Michelle Bisson
Art Director: Anahid Hamparian
Series Designer: Sonia Chaghatzbanian

Photo research by Marybeth Kavanagh

Cover photo by Darrell Gulin/Getty Images

The photographs in this book are used by permission and through the courtesy of: *Getty Images*: Jodi Cobb/ National Geographic, 2, 5; Phil Degginger, 23; Rick & Nora Bowers/Visuals Unlimited, 69(bottom); Keren Su, 85; *Cutcaster.com*: Henrik Lehne, 1, 2, 10,11, 28, 42, 43, 54, 55, 67, 72, 73, 85, 88; *Super Stock*: Dale Jorgenson, 6, 75; age fotostock, 26, 29, 69(top); Mark Conlin VWPics, 49; Pacific Stock, 50; James Urbach, 53; Hemis.fr, 59; Image Asset Management Ltd., 63, 65; Blend Images, 87; *Animals Animals/Earth Scenes*: Anne W. Rosenfeld, 9; *Alamy*: Picture Partners, 15; Frans Lanting Studio, 43; Malcolm Schuyl, 82; *AP Photo*: NASA, 20; *Corbis*: Dennis Kunkel Microscopy, Inc/Visuals Unlimited, 22; *Photo Researchers, Inc.*: David A. Hardy, 27; *The Image Works*: Jeff Greenberg, 31; B. Von Hoffmann/ClassicStock, 57; *Newscom*: CustomMedicalStock, 35, 37; ImagoStock, 80; *USGS, Colorado District*: John M. Evans, 41

Printed in Malaysia (T)
1 3 5 6 4 2

Contents

One
Our Place in Nature

Timing is everything when you visit the central California town called Moss Beach. Arrive at high tide, and you may wonder what the town's founders were thinking when they named it, for there is no sign of a beach in any direction. The Pacific Ocean swells up to meet the land, and waves break against high sandstone cliffs. But don't let disappointment drive you away. Follow the path that leads atop the cliffs. From there you'll have a sweeping view of the coastline, and if the season is right, you may see whales or dolphins offshore. Find a comfortable spot and settle in to observe. Over the next few hours the tide will slowly recede and expose a narrow strip of multicolored sand at the foot of the cliff. You might not find this miniature beach impressive at first, but keep watching. At Moss Beach the magic begins just where the sand ends.

During low tide, another world awaits discovery along this coastal California beach.

As the ebbing tide continues to draw away from the cliffs, it reveals a flat expanse of rock that stretches parallel to the beach and out toward the sea. From a distance these rocks look like the asphalt of an abandoned parking lot—cracked and lumpy, gray and barren. But the eager descent of gulls and shorebirds suggests that there's more there than meets the eye. An incoming stream of human visitors provides supporting evidence. They walk carefully but with purpose, stopping frequently to kneel and gaze at the rocks as if nothing more interesting existed in the world.

Make your way down to the beach, and you'll soon understand why people and birds are so attracted to these rocks. The lumps you noticed from above are actually clusters of mussels and barnacles. By remaining tightly anchored to the rock, these animals can resist the powerful force of waves. They open their shells to feed in water and, at low tide, close them tightly to avoid drying out. Between the shell beds sprout gardens of colorful algae that may resemble lettuce, tiny palm trees, or clumps of wet oak leaves. More commonly known as seaweed, the different forms of algae grasp the rock with rootlike holdfasts. Algae cannot obtain moisture or nutrients through the holdfasts as green plants do through their roots. But like green plants, algae produce their own food using carbon dioxide, water, and sunlight through the process of photosynthesis. Colorful snails with twisted shells inch through this unusual garden. You'll see similar shells wobbling and wandering across the rocks at a faster pace. Inside are hermit crabs, which adopt abandoned snail shells for their own protection.

More surprises are hidden in the crevices between rocks. Tide pools, which hold seawater, enable aquatic organisms to survive while the tide is out. Look for sea stars (or starfish), anemones, and sea urchins clinging to the walls of these natural aquariums. Sculpins and pricklebacks are small fish that often hide beneath shadowy overhangs to avoid the notice of feeding birds—and to escape the agile arms of hungry red octopuses. In turn, the fish feed on resident crabs and shrimp. But very few animals bother nudibranchs. If you are lucky enough to see one of these small sea slugs, notice its brilliant color and the feathery or bumpy surface of its skin. Most creatures in the tide pools have camouflage coloration that conceals them from predators. The nudibranch's flamboyant appearance, taking the opposite approach, is a warning that it is poisonous.

With time and patience you can find dozens more organisms in the rocky tide pools, including sea sponges, rock oysters, chitons, limpets, worms, kelp, corals, and even a type of flowering plant called surf grass. When you looked down from the cliffs at high tide, you might never have guessed that this bountiful habitat was here. Does it seem remarkable that these organisms can thrive in such an ever-changing and demanding environment? It is—yet this is just the nature of life on Earth.

The Changer and the Changed

It's not by chance that organisms in the Moss Beach tide pools have shells, holdfasts, camouflage, and poison. Physical features

Sea anemones and sea urchins are found in Moss Beach's intertidal zone.

It's Alive! Or Is It?

Ecologists divide components of the natural environment into two categories: abiotic and biotic. Abiotic factors include physical conditions of the environment such as sunlight and water. Biotic factors are alive. It's easy to tell that a deer, an oak tree, and a spider fit in this category. But think back to the first time you saw lichen on a rock or mold on cheese. Would you have known these things were alive if someone hadn't told you?

How can you distinguish whether something in the environment is biotic or abiotic? Biologists have identified seven characteristics that define cellular life. Living things have these characteristics:

- They have a complex organization, containing one or more cells.
- They acquire and use energy.
- They show the capacity to grow and develop.
- They reproduce.
- They maintain a stable internal environment (by regulating waste removal, pH, water concentration, and other factors) in a process called homeostasis.
- They interact with the external environment.
- They are adapted to the environment and have the capacity to evolve.

Viral units are considered biotic, but they are not cells. They cannot move, grow, or reproduce outside of living host cells. Some abiotic factors partially fulfill the requirements to be considered biotic. Mineral crystals grow. Fire "eats" other materials and spreads. A refrigerator uses energy and has controls to maintain its temperature and humidity. But these are not biotic because they do not meet all seven criteria at once.

What about a deer's antlers, the skin left behind when a spider molts, or the oaken door in your house? These objects were once part of a living thing, so they are still biotic. Fossil fuels are made from ancient plants and microscopic animals. These organisms died in ancient swamps and seas. Over time they were buried and subjected to intense heat and pressure, causing chemical changes that left coal, oil, or natural gas. Would you consider fossil fuels to be biotic or abiotic? While there is some disagreement about this among experts because fossil fuels undergo such dramatic chemical change during their formation, the fact that they originated from living sources is a good argument that they are biotic.

and behaviors that improve an organism's chance of survival are called adaptations. Adaptations, which allow organisms to meet their basic life needs in the conditions and resources of their environment, require long periods of time to develop. The most crucial adaptations involve acquiring energy, nutrients, and water; maintaining a stable internal body temperature; exchanging gases such as oxygen and carbon dioxide; and finding sufficient living space. Many organisms also have adaptations for self-defense or for competing with rivals for mates and for food, territory, and other resources.

Living things shape their physical environment as well as being affected by it. In the tide pools, barnacles scrape into rock as they attach. Algae and surf grass create shade that reduces water temperature nearby. They also alter the chemical balance of the water when they take in carbon dioxide and produce oxygen during photosynthesis. When hermit crabs eat dead animals in the pools, these scavengers begin the process of decomposition that returns nutrients to the environment for reuse. If you visit tide pools in Hawaii, India, or anywhere else in the world, you'll find collections of species with adaptations similar to those at Moss Beach. Choose any other setting—a desert, a coral reef, or even a square of grass in your backyard. Observe it closely, and you'll notice that the resident organisms interact with each other and are adapted for their environment. These settings are known as ecosystems.

Ecologists are scientists who study the interactions between organisms and the environment. They have determined that ecosystems exist on scales from huge to miniscule and from simple to complex. A tropical rain forest covering an entire country may be considered an ecosystem. A cornfield is a human-made ecosystem, as is a city. Even your body is an ecosystem, home to millions of bacteria and other microscopic organisms that have adapted to life on (or in) *you*.

Human Adaptations

We humans are also well adapted for our way of life. Because we are usually active in the daytime, the retina of the human eye has an especially large number of cells called cones, which

12

are sensitive to color. Cones are absent in nocturnal animals. The ability to walk upright was a great advantage to early hominids (members of the human family tree), in which this trait appeared approximately 5.8 million years ago. From an upright stance, hominids could see over greater distances. The upright stance also enabled the forelimbs to be used to carry children, food, and other things. This change in posture was no small event; it required modifications of the spine, pelvis, and leg bones. Another valuable adaptation is found in the hand. While all primates have an opposable thumb, bones in the human hand are shaped differently to allow a greater range of motion. Unlike other primates, humans can grasp and manipulate even very small objects with their hands.

Despite these advantageous traits, we humans also appear more vulnerable than other animals. We have no significant means of self-protection: no covering of hair, no fangs, no claws, no source of poison. The real key to human survival is our large brain. Rapid growth in the brain size of our hominid predecessors enabled them to produce increasingly sophisticated stone tools. They also learned to produce fire and in many other ways to alter the environment according to their needs.

It is easy to recognize these adaptations but harder to see ourselves as part of nature. A lot of our time is spent indoors. Cars and airplanes allow us to travel to distant places in a matter of hours rather than crossing the land slowly, as people did just a few generations ago. Look around the house—in the bedroom closet, the living room, the fridge. Chances are, most of what you see is manufactured. Moreover, a substantial proportion of your belongings—including the food—probably originated in locations hundreds or thousands of miles from your home.

No matter how little time we spend outdoors, we are part of an ecosystem. Clean water, air, soil, and nutrients—all of these are provided by organisms and cycles in the natural world. Natural cycles regulate Earth's climate. We rely on a food chain that begins with plants. Animals pollinate many of our crops, and they control pests that would otherwise eat our food supplies or transmit illness. Living things are also

an important source of medicines. Ecologists and economists have made attempts to quantify the value of these services to humanity, but the connections are so complex that numbers fail to express them. The spiritual, psychological, and artistic inspiration people receive from nature is also priceless.

It Goes Both Ways

Just as we depend on nature, our actions impact the health of the environment and the ability of natural systems to properly function. Since the mid–twentieth century, ecologists and other scientists have noticed a decline in biodiversity and in the function of many ecosystems. Much of this change is the result of human population growth. In 1800 the world population was approximately one billion. It exceeded 6.8 billion in 2010.

The ever-increasing human population demands great amounts of food, water, and other natural resources such as wood and metals. It also creates tremendous volumes of waste that have to be disposed of by burning or storage in landfills. The term *ecological footprint* refers to the amount of land and sea needed to supply these needs for one individual over the period of a year. According to the World Wildlife Fund's *Living Planet Report 2008*, which reviews nations worldwide, only the United Arab Emirates has a larger ecological footprint than the United States (keeping in mind that the footprint is an average and that within a nation, each person behaves differently). Because of their high levels of consumption, people in wealthier regions tend to have the biggest footprints. Population size also plays a role. Although each individual in China has a small footprint compared with an American's, China's population is so much larger that its cumulative impact is just as great. Together the United States and China use 21 percent of Earth's natural resources. Although the rate of population growth has begun to decrease, the number of humans continues to climb and may reach 9 billion by 2050. If ecological footprints remain large, the result will be increasing food and water shortages along with the unsustainable use of natural resources.

As the world's population grows, the stress placed on Earth's natural resources increases.

Several international organizations have identified the impact of human population and overconsumption on biodiversity. They recognize that human alteration of the environment has far-reaching effects, even in seemingly disconnected ecosystems. For example, some migratory ducks and other waterfowl spend the winter on shallow coastal bays. In spring they move inland to sheltered marshes to breed. These populations are often left "homeless" when wetlands are drained for use as farm fields and new housing developments. In tropical rain forests the high density of trees results in a buildup of clouds as water released by the trees condenses in the hot air. These clouds often produce local afternoon rain showers (hence the term "tropical rain forest"). Because the clouds reflect some of the incoming sunlight, there is a reduction in temperature over

the forest. The rain not only hydrates the forest but also further decreases air temperature—at least for a while. As winds push some of these clouds beyond their point of origin, they provide water to other regions. Deforestation is thus a doubly damaging process. It not only depletes biodiversity but may also alter local and regional weather patterns.

In 1992 the United Nations held an international meeting called Earth Summit in Rio de Janeiro, Brazil. Its goal was to seek sustainable methods of obtaining resources while protecting the environment. Representatives of 178 nations discussed a variety of issues, including

- reduction of air, water, and soil pollution;
- research to identify and implement alternative sources of energy to supplement and replace fossil fuels (oil, natural gas, and coal), which produce emissions that lead to air pollution (with related human health problems), acid rain, and climate change;
- improved access to clean water in poor and drought-stricken regions of the world;
- decreasing human impacts on natural ecosystems from development, logging, hunting and fishing, and other activities.

The Earth Summit generated high hopes for a reduction in humans' environmental impact. Yet these goals were not easy to achieve. In 2000 the United Nations secretary-general, Kofi Annan, asked scientists worldwide to collaborate on a project evaluating the impact of ongoing ecosystem damage on humans, now and in the future. He wanted their recommendations on how to better conserve and sustain the resources available to us. This project, called the Millennium Ecosystem Assessment (MEA), revealed that the "rapidly growing demands for food, fresh water, timber, fiber and fuel . . . has resulted in a substantial and largely irreversible loss in the diversity of life on Earth." MEA scientists list five areas of concern that require particular attention:

- Habitat change, loss, and fragmentation. People clear land for housing, crops, and livestock grazing and to obtain lumber and firewood. Smaller pieces of wilderness support less diversity and reduce the ability of natural systems to function.

- Invasive alien species. Alien species (also called introduced species) are those that are transported by humans from one region into another where they do not naturally occur. This movement may be intentional or accidental. In general, alien species have no natural predators or other controls in the new setting. As a result, they spread well and may compete against or kill native species.

- Introduced pathogens (a subcategory of alien species). Pathogens are microscopic organisms such as bacteria, viruses, and parasites that can cause disease. Introduced pathogens may lead to disease outbreaks among humans but also can affect wildlife and plants, including crops.

- Overexploitation. Each organism has a role in its ecosystem. Yet large numbers of many species are collected for food, medicine, the pet trade, paper production and other wood products, and more. Overexploitation can lead to extinction of species.

- Climate change. Fossil fuels (oil, natural gas, and coal) have been burned at an increasing rate during the past century, changing the concentration of carbon dioxide in the atmosphere. Other industrial chemicals released into the atmosphere add to this problem, potentially altering Earth's patterns of temperature, precipitation, ice storage, and sea level. There is potential for change in all of Earth's ecosystems.

The MEA also notes that the impact of humans on biodiversity may change over time. Our impact should be assessed frequently, and our responses must adapt accordingly.

The World Wildlife Fund's *Living Planet Index 2008* adds a sixth, related concern to the list: pollution. Among the sources of pollution are chemicals released by fossil-fuel burning and industrial manufacturing, agricultural fertilizers, and sewage.

The effects of these threats can be seen almost everywhere—even in the tide pools at Moss Beach. Pollution of the water, overexploitation by shell collectors, habitat change in the surrounding community, and even climate change have taken their toll on this little ecosystem. It is easy to feel overwhelmed in the face of such environmental damage. And it's true that the momentum created by poor choices in the past may result in some ongoing damages. Yet there is hope. Conscientious efforts by scientists and the public have reversed serious environmental problems in the past.

In 1970, researchers visited California's Channel Islands to check on nesting brown pelicans. They found that the population, which had once numbered in the thousands, was down to three hundred nesting pairs. In their nests the scientists found few or no eggs. Most of the eggs they did find were cracked. The birds were unable to raise young that year and abandoned the colony. The cause was discovered to be DDT, an insecticide chemical widely used to kill crop pests. For decades DDT was made in a Los Angeles factory, and wastes were dumped directly into the ocean. Microscopic plankton in the water absorbed the chemical. Plankton are the basis of the marine food web. They are eaten by invertebrate animals, which in turn are consumed by fish. DDT is not soluble in water, but it does begin to break down in oil. DDT had become stored in the fatty tissues of many organisms, and large concentrations were found in organisms higher on the food chain. The brown pelicans had an especially high exposure because their diet consists of large numbers of fish. DDT and its byproducts blocked calcium deposition in the birds' bodies; lack of calcium caused their eggshells to thin. The insecticide was banned from use in 1972. At the same time, placement on the Endangered Species List protected pelicans from other risks such as hunting, egg collection, and habitat destruction.

The results began to show within a few years. By the 1990s approximately five thousand nests were counted each year on the Channel Islands. Although the population continues to fluctuate somewhat in response to environmental conditions and human inputs, such as water pollution, it was considered stable enough to be removed from the Endangered Species List in November 2009.

Pelicans might not seem important to your life, but a gaping hole in the ozone layer would be. Ozone is a gas with three atoms of oxygen per molecule. In the upper atmosphere, ozone forms a thin layer that absorbs as much as 97 to 99 percent of the ultraviolet (UV) light that reaches Earth from the sun. High levels of UV radiation can cause genetic damage and cancer, so the ozone layer is crucial to the health of living things on Earth. In the 1980s scientists discovered that the ozone layer had become thinner over the continent of Antarctica. Increasing use of chlorofluorocarbon chemicals, or CFCs, in aerosol cans, packaging, insulation, and cooling systems had led to the formation of this ozone hole. Prior to this discovery, CFCs were considered safe for humans and the environment. But scientists concerned about the ozone hole found that CFCs rose into the atmosphere, where solar radiation and cold temperatures caused them to break down. Chlorine atoms released from CFCs attacked ozone.

Because CFCs came from nations worldwide, an international agreement called the Montreal Protocol was written to deal with the issue. Passed in 1987, it asked the world's industrialized nations to discontinue use of CFCs and related chemicals that can cause depletion of the ozone layer. Its recovery will take time, because ozone-depleting chemicals can remain in the atmosphere for decades. But there are promising signs of recovery. Scientists measure the ozone hole when it reappears over Antarctica each year. It remains large, but the density of ozone molecules has increased since 1998. According to the U.S. Environmental Protection Agency, it may return to normal levels by 2075.

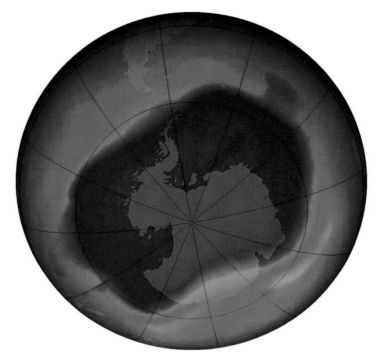

The blue and purple colors in this image represent the region over the Antarctic with the least amount of ozone. This area measured 10.6 million square miles (27.5 million square kilometers) on the date this image was photographed, September 24, 2006.

These examples prove that giving up is not the solution. It seems that we can make a difference when we work with nature rather than against it. One key is to recognize that living things in ecosystems are interdependent. The naturalist John Muir noticed this interdependence in the 1860s as he walked through the lushly forested mountains of California. "When we try to pick out anything by itself," he wrote, "we find it hitched to everything else in the universe." With this perspective, ecosystems might be described as living machines. Each part has a separate value and "job," but only when they work together does the machine function efficiently. Learning how the cogs and wheels of our living Earth fit together gives us a chance to preserve the integrity of all the services they provide.

Two

The Variety of Life

Biologists have so far described and named approximately 2 million living species, and they agree that many more are yet to be found. The exact total remains unclear, with most estimates ranging from 5 to 30 million. Species are classified into three domains—Bacteria, Archaea, or Eukarya—on the basis of differences in their cell types, the number of cells they contain, and the ways they obtain energy.

All living things have chromosomes, genetic material that controls the growth, reproduction, and functioning of cells and whole organisms. Bacterial and archaeal microorganisms have prokaryotic cells, in which the chromosome (usually just one, arranged in a loop) floats freely in the fluid of the cell. This arrangement seems to be the most ancient. Eukaryotic chromosomes are twisted in a helix shape and are held inside a membrane, forming a nucleus.

Bacteria are unicellular—that is, the body contains just one cell, though the cells of bacteria range in size. Some are autotrophic, the Greek roots of which mean "self-feeding." Autotrophs make their own food using energy from sunlight (photosynthesis) or chemicals, such as sulfur (chemosynthesis). Others are heterotrophic ("other-feeding"), or unable to make their own food.

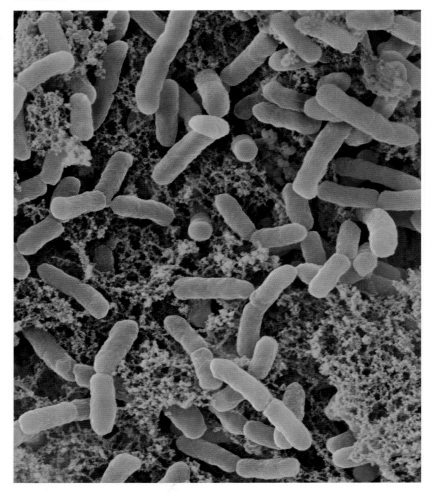

Chlorobium tepidum bacteria are thermophilic and grow in dense mats over hot springs.

Heterotrophs must ingest other organisms or nutrients to survive. The archaea meet these same criteria—they are unicellular and may be autotrophic or heterotrophic. But in most other ways archaea are as different from bacteria as you are. This group includes species that are adapted to some of Earth's most extreme environments. Different groups are found in boiling volcanic geysers, such as those at Yellowstone National Park; in the frigid ice at the poles; in the deep ocean, where there may be little or no oxygen; and in places where it is excessively salty, acidic, or alkaline.

Most eukaryotes are multicellular; they run the gamut in size from microscopic algae to massive blue whales and redwood trees. The Eukarya domain includes four kingdoms: Fungi, Animalia, Plantae, and Protoctista. Protoctista is a catch-all group of organisms; unlike the other eukaryotes, its members are not separately classified because they share important characteristics. Many are microscopic, and some are multicellular, but that's about where the similarities end. Protoctists may be heterotrophic or use photosynthesis. They are common in freshwater, oceans, and soil, but some groups are parasites that live inside other organisms.

Fungi include molds, yeast, rusts, and mushroom-producing club fungi. Occurring in many environments—including soil and water and the bodies of other organisms—fungi are heterotrophs but do not eat. Instead, they produce chemical enzymes that cause food items to break down into simpler molecules that can be absorbed and digested.

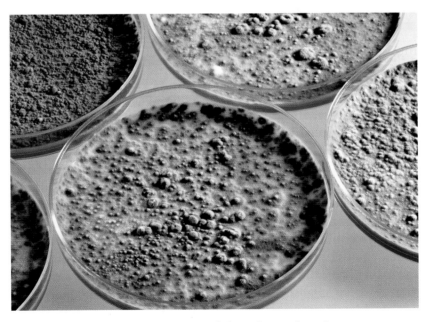

Fungi, such as molds, are members of the Eukarya domain.

The animal kingdom is divided into many classes. Informally, they fall into two groups. Invertebrates are animals without backbones, such as sponges, jellyfish, many types of worms, mollusks (from snails to squid), hard-bodied crustaceans (including lobsters and spiders), insects, and echinoderms (such as sea stars). Vertebrate animals are less diverse but perhaps more familiar: fishes, amphibians, reptiles, birds, and mammals.

The simplest plants are mosses and related species. They have none of the structures usually associated with plants—no stems, leaves, or roots. Lacking these, there is no efficient way for water or nutrients to move through the body and nothing that holds the organism upright. For this reason, mosses grow low to the ground. Vascular plants include ferns, conifers, and flowering plants. These plants, far more complex in structure, have networks of specialized cells that conduct fluids, much as the animal vascular system moves blood. Like mosses, ferns rely on water to spread their spores for reproduction. Conifers, such as pine and cypress trees, have seeds in cones. Flowering plants produce many different kinds of fruits to distribute their seeds.

Life Abounds

Biodiversity reflects much more than simple species diversity in an ecosystem. As we've seen, species not only live together, they also interact. Therefore biodiversity reflects the number of species in an ecosystem plus the connections between them.

Imagine a local park that has a parking lot, sports fields, and a wooded area with hiking trails. The parking lot may have been landscaped with some plants. These plants attract a small number of animals, and soil always contains a variety of organisms. But most of this area is covered in asphalt and contributes little to biodiversity. The playing fields look nice and green. However, turf contains only one or two species of grass, accompanied by a few dandelions or other hardy weeds that have snuck in. There may be visitors such as birds, but the greatest diversity is in the soil, where invertebrates and microorganisms do their work.

The forest, by contrast, is quite complex. It contains several species of trees that make up the canopy; that is, the highest level of plant growth. Below the canopy are the small trees and shrubs in the understory. Low-growing plants hug the ground, while a layer of leaf litter and other decaying matter forms a fourth layer on the forest floor. Other organisms are spread throughout the layers, but this distribution is not random. Many cluster around specific resources—fungi and insects are often found in rotting logs, frogs and turtles near water, and so forth. Birds and mammals may use several levels of the forest for food sources and nesting sites. Each population is adapted for its niche, or role, in the ecosystem. In this park scenario, the forest has far more niches than the playing field. The parking lot has the fewest niches of all. More niches equals greater diversity.

Tropical rain forests are the movie stars of the natural world, celebrated as the most exotic and exciting ecosystems on the planet. This reputation is not without merit, as Panama's Barro Colorado Island shows. Although it is just one-fourth the size of New York's Manhattan Island, scientists have found more than 1,300 plant species on Barro Colorado, along with 381 different birds and thousands of insect species—including 225 types of ants. Although tropical rain forests are found on only 7 percent of Earth's land surface, some estimates suggest that they may contain 90 percent of all species. Biodiversity here is increased by endemism; rather than being widespread, many species occur only regionally and nowhere else on Earth.

Other areas, such as the polar regions and the deep sea, have been considered too harsh to support such diverse ecosystems. However, new surveys are forcing scientists to rethink their ideas about how biodiversity is distributed across the planet. Take the South Orkney Islands, located close to Antarctica and half a world away from the lush, tropical wilderness of Barro Colorado. Around the South Orkneys air and water temperatures remain frigid even in summer, and most of the land is covered by glacial ice. Yet a 2008 survey found more than 1,200 species on and around these islands—

**Diversity abounds in rain forests. Here a red-eyed tree frog perches
on a heliconia plant. Many of these organisms occur nowhere else
in the world.**

from penguins and sea urchins along the shoreline to worms
and sea stars living on the seafloor at depths of 4,900 feet
(1,500 meters). Biodiversity "hot spots" such as Madagascar,
Sri Lanka, and the islands of the Caribbean are also regions
with high endemism.

It's also becoming clear that ecosystems develop above and
within Earth as well as on it. Scientists have found that pollen,
algae, and bacteria are common in the atmosphere as much as

4 miles (6.4 kilometers) above Earth's surface. These micro-organisms and plant spores may even be involved in the formation of snowflakes and raindrops. Bacteria have also been discovered in tiny puddles of volcanically heated water that are trapped inside rocks more than 2 miles (3.2 km) below-ground. When submersible vehicles dived to the deepest part of the Pacific Ocean, near Guam, scientists found bacterial communities surrounding vents where superheated water and sulfuric chemicals jet up from beneath the ocean's crust. But the bacteria are not alone. In the inky darkness around these vents—at a depth of 35,800 feet (10,912 m)—are shrimp, slug-like sea cucumbers, and tall tube worms. The existence of these ecosystems suggests that life is tenacious and will take hold wherever resources are available.

Ecosystems can form deep beneath the seas, such as at black smoker vents. Tube worms, mollusks, crustaceans, and fish thrive thanks to bacteria that form the base of the food web.

BioBlitz!

People live in a wide variety of ecosystems. Some continue to rely exclusively on what they can hunt and gather from the land, just as our ancestors did thousands of years ago. Farming remains an important way of life for many others. Increasing numbers of people live in towns and cities that seem far from nature. But anywhere we live, however we live, humans play a role in nature.

Over the past decade or more, scientists and citizens have been eager to find out just how diverse human ecosystems are. The BioBlitz is a twenty-four-hour biological survey conducted by experts and volunteers of all ages. Participants look for every kind of living thing in the survey area, from large birds and mammals to microorganisms in soil and water. New Yorkers identified 479 species in Central Park during a 2006 survey event. The 2007 BioBlitz, held in Washington, DC's, Rock Creek Park (on the edge of the U.S. capital city), turned up 661 species. Surveyors for the 2008 BioBlitz in North Shore, New Zealand (near the city of Aukland), topped both of these results. Working in a nature reserve less than 3 percent the size of Central Park, they found 946 species.

BioBlitz results show that parks in or near cities can be refuges for biodiversity. However, these green spaces are often cut off from other natural ecosystems. Biodiversity improves when ecosystems are large, complex, and interconnected.

Fragile

Despite its tenacity, life on Earth is fragile. Even the most biodiverse ecosystems are vulnerable to overexploitation. This includes hunting, fishing, and harvesting of resources such as wood and minerals. This happens on different scales. Throughout the world there continue to be populations that live close to the land and rely on it for their survival. They need meat, plant foods, and wood for fuel. This type of harvesting may be sustainable when populations are small. As human communities grow, however, the demand for materials increases and may impact local ecosystems.

In the tropical forests of Africa's Congo Basin live our closest animal relatives—chimpanzees and gorillas. Yet their populations are under tremendous stress. Logging and mining remove forest habitat required by these secretive species. The production of charcoal is an equal threat. Trees are cut and the wood burned down to make charcoal, a primary source of fuel in the homes of Central African people. People have even begun

Overexploitation of Africa's Congo Basin has become a threat to one of its inhabitants, the lowland gorilla.

to produce charcoal from trees in the region's protected areas—including Virunga National Park. Virunga is Africa's oldest national park, protecting more than one-quarter of the world's remaining population of mountain gorillas. Rangers are constantly on patrol to keep charcoal makers out of the park. Recognizing that poor local people resort to such extremes because they require fuel, energy experts are seeking other options for them. One alternative fuel is briquettes, blocks of pressed material made from grasses, leaves, and other waste materials that can be collected without damaging the ecosystem.

Local people may have an impact on their ecosystem, but outsiders do even more damage. The Millennium Ecosystem Assessment reports that nearly $160 billion per year changes hands in the trade of wild plants and animals. Animals are collected for meat, fur, and leather; as pets; and for use in the production of traditional medicines. Plants may be sold live; timber is used for a variety of products, including paper, construction, furniture, and musical instruments.

Overexploitation impacts every type of ecosystem, on land and in water. In its 2008 report *The State of the World's Fisheries and Aquaculture*, the Food and Agriculture Organization of the United Nations (FAO) indicated that about 28 percent of the world's fish stocks were overexploited, a trend that began in the 1970s. "The maximum wild capture fisheries potential from the world's oceans has probably been reached," warn the authors, "and a more closely controlled approach to fisheries management is required." The FAO also reviewed the state of forests in 229 regions of the planet. Experts studied biodiversity, the availability of productive resources for human use, ecological health of the forests, and other factors. They found that between 2000 and 2005, an average of 18 million acres (7.3 million hectares) of forest was cut down each year—an area equivalent in size to the state of Maine.

Deforestation has multiple repercussions. Tree roots take hold deep in the soil and prevent the tree from blowing away. Intact soil allows water to soak though the ground and recharge local supplies of groundwater. Removing these trees leads to erosion. Trees and other plants take up large amounts

The Talladega National Forest in Tuscaloosa, Alabama, has been affected by deforestation by the logging industry.

of carbon dioxide (CO_2) from the atmosphere and convert it to carbohydrates through the process of photosynthesis. Deforestation reduces the ability of natural systems to remove CO_2 from the environment. Deforestation is not always intended to harvest wood; often the forest is burned to clear land for cattle grazing or farming. The FAO estimates that Earth's forests hold 50 percent more carbon dioxide than the concentration in the atmosphere. When wood is burned, its stored carbon is rapidly released.

Carbon dioxide is a greenhouse gas. Others include water vapor, methane, nitrous oxide, ozone, and a variety of man-made chemicals. Earth has always had greenhouse gases. They insulate the planet by trapping some of the heat that comes from the sun. Excess concentrations of natural greenhouse gases and the addition of man-made varieties cause an increase in temperature that may change global climate. Over the next century climate change is predicted to cause droughts in some regions, more severe weather in others, and loss of sea ice and glaciers.

Increased temperatures may also warm the world's oceans; a resulting rise in sea level may contribute to a change in ecosystems to which marine organisms are adapted.

Currently the highest rates of deforestation are in South America, Africa, and Asia. These tropical regions host high levels of diversity. For example, the nation of Brazil has 7,780 species of trees. Among the trees live unimaginable numbers of other plants, invertebrates (especially insects), birds, and other magnificent animals. Loss of species is tragic, for each plays a role in its ecosystem. Once a population is gone, it cannot be recovered. But there is more to consider as ecosystems decline. These are not just distant places—they are the machines that sustain life on Earth.

Three
Energy and Matter in Ecosystems

Ecosystems are not random collections of organisms. Ecologists have identified several levels of complexity in ecosystems and recognize that different types of interactions occur at each level. The simplest level is the individual. Individuals are part of a population—a group made up of the same species. In March 2010 almost 309 million people lived in the United States. The 534 residents of Achille, Oklahoma, also represent a population. A study can look at the global population of a species or at more localized segments of it, so long as the parameters are defined in advance.

All of the populations of species living in an area form a community. Add the abiotic factors of the environment, and a community becomes an ecosystem. Ecosystems are subdivisions of biomes. These large geographical areas share similar climate and vegetation patterns. Tide pools are part of the intertidal zone, a biome located where land meets the sea. The central California coastline, including the land above the Moss Beach tide pools in the town of Moss Beach, lies within the Mediterranean forest, woodland, and scrub biome.

This biome also occurs around the Mediterranean Sea (for which it was named), in southern Australia, along the Pacific coast of Chile, and at the southernmost tip of South Africa. These five regions are geographically widespread, but they have such similar environmental conditions—poor soils, seasonal rains followed by dry periods, and frequent fires—that the resident plants developed similar adaptations. A total of fourteen terrestrial (land-based) biomes have been defined in a system devised by the World Wildlife Fund. This system also delineates ten marine (oceanic) biomes and seven in freshwater.

The broadest level of all is the biosphere, which encompasses any part of Earth where life can exist—from the abyssal depths of the ocean to the swirling currents of the atmosphere. It sounds like a huge expanse, but in reality the biosphere is a small space to contain so many living things. Ecologist Barry Commoner once described the biosphere as a "thin, life-supporting skin" around the planet. So far as we know, this is the only place in the solar system capable of supporting life.

Sunlight = Energy

Think back to the last time you saw a wild animal—a bird, a squirrel, an insect. What was it doing? Chances are, it was searching for or eating food. A large part of any individual's life is spent obtaining the next meal (or manufacturing it, in the case of autotrophs such as plants and algae). Likewise, the fundamental interactions in any ecosystem involve food. Individuals compete for it. Populations adapt to better obtain it. Energy flows through the system as one organism eats another.

In most cases, energy in an ecosystem begins with the sun. Certain types of organisms—including plants and some members of the Bacteria, Archaea, and Protoctista kingdoms—are called producers because they can make their own food from abiotic components in the environment. The ingredients of photosynthesis are carbon dioxide, water, and sunlight. Carbon dioxide is a gas found in the atmosphere and in water. Plants obtain CO_2 through small holes in their leaves. Water is drawn in through their roots. Among less complex producers these substances diffuse into the body through the surrounding cell membrane.

The key to photosynthesis is chlorophyll, a green pigment in the cells that absorbs sunlight. In the first step of photosynthesis, sunlight is captured by chlorophyll and used to split water (H_2O) molecules into separate atoms of hydrogen and oxygen. Hydrogen ions are carried into the next step of photosynthesis and combined with carbon dioxide. Oxygen is released into the atmosphere as waste. The primary product of these reactions is glucose, a type of simple sugar molecule.

To release the energy in glucose, plants and other organisms use a process called cellular respiration. Glucose molecules are first broken into pyruvic acid. This breakdown releases energy used to produce two types of molecules, called ATP and NADH. In the presence of oxygen, pyruvic acids can be further broken down to produce CO_2, water, and energy to form more ATP. ATP is a carrier of energy, which can be used to do work in the cell. Carbon dioxide is the waste product of cellular respiration.

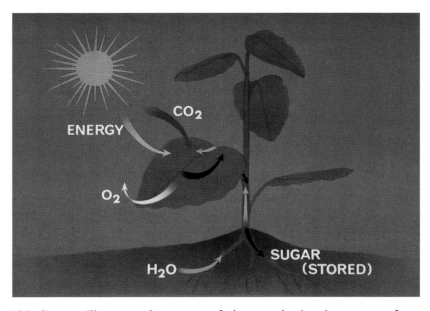

This diagram illustrates the process of photosynthesis, where energy from the sun is transformed into stored food energy in the form of sugars.

If there is no oxygen available, some organisms can break down glucose using fermentation instead of respiration to produce lactic acid or alcohol plus CO_2. In both cases a smaller (but still useful) amount of ATP is also made.

Respiration and photosynthesis are complementary processes. They form a cycle that constantly moves CO_2, water, and oxygen between living things and the environment. But this was not always the case. In its early stages Earth had a lot of carbon dioxide and little free oxygen. The first organisms were cyanobacteria (a type of Archaea) that, by photosynthesizing, added oxygen to the atmosphere. By 1.5 billion years ago (more than 3 billion years after Earth's formation) the concentration of atmospheric oxygen had stabilized. Under these new conditions, those first simple organisms began to branch out into more complex forms that eventually led to the biodiversity we see on Earth today.

Links in the Chain

Plants use sugars for growth, maintenance, and reproduction. Measure the growth of a plant in your house or garden. Over time its stem becomes taller and wider and the roots longer, and new leaves sprout. Plants also store sugars in seeds, fruits, and tubers. Seeds need a supply of energy to allow the rapid growth of a new plant. Fruits contain sugars to attract animals. Bulbs are fattened extensions of the stem that are held underground, serving as the plant's food reserves in winter or in times when nutrients are in short supply from photosynthesis.

Sit down in the garden on a warm summer day and you'll see that many animal populations take advantage of the food stored in plants. Caterpillars munch on leaves, while many beetles prefer tree bark. Birds feast on fruit, often gobbling seeds and all. The seeds are later deposited in new places—complete with a built-in source of fertilizer. Squirrels must crack open the hard shells of the nuts they gather to reach the nutritious meat inside. Gophers tunnel beneath the soil in search of tubers and bulbs. This passage of energy from plants to animals is called a food chain. But the food chain doesn't stop here. Toads snap caterpillars off the undersides of leaves at night. Woodpeckers hammer holes in the bark to find beetle larvae. Local cats hunt gophers. A raccoon eats fruit, but it's just as likely to make a meal of birds' eggs.

Ecologists describe food chains to follow the flow of energy from one organism to the next. In reality, the feeding relationships between populations in a community are more like webs, because most organisms eat more than one type of food.

Food-web diagrams, showing the connections between organisms, are like road maps. Each feeding strategy is called a trophic level. As the source of energy for the system, producers are placed at the base of the diagram. Primary consumers eat producers. A grasshopper is a primary consumer because it eats grass leaves. Primary consumers may also be called herbivores. The garter snake that eats the grasshopper is a secondary consumer, or carnivore. The term "carnivore" can be confusing, however, because it also applies to the hawk that catches the snake. It's more accurate to say that the hawk is a third-level, or tertiary, consumer.

The multitude of interlinking food chains in an ecosystem form a food web.

Like the raccoon in the garden, some organisms fill more than one trophic level. These are the omnivores. American robins are a good example. Robins are first-level consumers when eating berries but become second-level consumers when they catch grasshoppers. Black bears are also omnivores; their diet includes animal prey and scavenged meat. Scavengers eat dead organisms that they have not killed. For some animals, like black bears, scavenged food makes up only part of their diet. Bald eagles get a lot of their nutrition from scavenged meat, but they also capture fish and ducks. You will often see crows pecking at roadkill, but the eggs and nestlings of smaller birds are another part of their diet. At the other extreme, vultures show no interest in hunting. Carcasses provide their entire food source.

Invertebrates such as beetles, wood lice, millipedes, earthworms, and slugs belong to a group of scavengers called detritivores. Depending on the species, they consume dead animals, animal waste, or dead plants. As detritivores eat, organic matter is shredded into smaller pieces. Decomposers can then move in. These organisms break organic material down to its most basic chemical parts. Bacteria decompose animal remains, while fungi work on plants. Decomposers do not eat food and digest it internally. Instead, they produce enzymes that cause matter to break apart. They absorb the elements needed for nutrition and energy; the remainder is left in the environment for later reuse.

It's rare to find food chains that have many more than five levels (aside from scavenging and decomposition). There's a good reason for this. An organism takes in a lot of food in its lifetime. But much of this food is used up. Life is hard work! The transformation of food to energy and energy to life processes creates heat. Excess heat is lost to the environment; the organism cannot use it again. In physics this situation is called entropy and is described by the second law of thermodynamics: when energy is converted from one form to another, the amount of useful energy decreases. On average, only about 10 percent of the energy from one trophic level gets passed to the next.

In other words, when a grasshopper eats grass, it receives one-tenth the amount of energy that the grass made during photosynthesis. The snake gets one-tenth of the grasshopper's stored energy—just one-hundredth of what was in the grass. This situation can be depicted as a pyramid. The wide base represents producers, with the most energy. At successive trophic levels the amount of energy decreases, so the pyramid narrows. The tip of the pyramid symbolizes the highest-level consumer. Very little of the original energy made available by producers remains at this level.

Think back to the garden. Did you ever notice that there are far more plants than insects? In turn, there are more insects than birds. This is true in any food chain or ecosystem. The amount of biomass, or biological weight, decreases at each trophic level in approximate proportion to the loss of energy.

Food webs support every living thing on Earth. But they are easily disrupted. This sometimes happens as a result of overexploitation, as in the oceans and forests. Australia's cane toad exemplifies what can happen when people introduce species into a food web. A small group of cane toads was transported from Hawaii to Australia in 1935. Sugarcane farmers hoped that the toads would eat beetles that had been killing their plants. The toads proved useless in this capacity. But they ate many other types of insects, including the bees that pollinate native Australian plants. Cane toads even ate birds' eggs, frogs, and small mammals. Because of a toxin in the toad's body that protects it from predators, the cane toad has thrived. Today the species is so widespread that it is difficult to control.

Ecologist Aldo Leopold described an opposite effect in his book *A Sand County Almanac*. He and his friends came upon a pack of wolves while hunting. Like most people in the mid–twentieth century, they considered wolves to be pests—a threat to human safety, reckless killers of livestock, and competitors for deer. The hunters killed the wolves. Leopold later regretted this decision; he became an advocate for predators

and for ethical hunting. He explained what happened after the wolves were killed:

> I have watched the face of many a newly wolfless mountain, and seen the south-facing slopes wrinkle with a maze of new deer trails. I have seen every edible bush and seedling browsed, first to anaemic desuetude, and then to death. I have seen every edible tree defoliated to the height of a saddle-horn. . . . In the end the starved bones of the hoped-for deer herd, dead of its own too-much, bleach with the bones of the dead sage, or molder under the high-lined junipers.

"Desuetude" is a state of being unused. Leopold's description reveals what happens when predators are removed from an ecosystem. Herbivores overpopulate and eventually overexploit their food resources. Left with no food, they die. Since Leopold wrote that essay in the 1940s, biologists have learned that wolves typically kill sick, elderly, or very young prey. Rather than harming herds of deer, elk, and caribou, this strengthens the population. In general, predators—sharks, hawks, snakes, and others—take only what they need to survive. That's a good lesson for humans.

The Cycles of Life

Energy flows through food chains thanks to a constantly renewed amount of sunlight. But Earth has a finite amount of matter, which must be recycled in ecosystems. When decomposers break down organic material, chemical elements return to the environment. The most common is nitrogen, which makes up about 78 percent of the atmosphere. Oxygen accounts for 21 percent of the atmosphere, and carbon dioxide just 0.03 percent. Other elements, such as phosphorus and sulfur, are essential for life but occur in trace amounts.

Carbon is considered the defining element of life. Photosynthesis converts CO_2 gas to sugars, which are broken down again by respiration or decomposition. Carbon may remain in certain parts of the environment for long periods of time.

The ocean is a significant reservoir of carbon dioxide; each living thing also has a supply. The amount of carbon moving between living things and the environment has been consistent over many periods of Earth's history, but environmental conditions can alter this balance. A long ice age delays decomposition. Forest fires release carbon that has been stored in trees for decades or centuries. Fossil fuels also contain ancient carbon. Burning fossil fuels in vehicles, power plants, and factories rapidly increases the amount of carbon dioxide in the atmosphere and has been linked to changes in global climate over the past century.

On average, 60 percent of human body weight is from water. Every living thing needs water, and all cells contain it. Water moves between living things, the land, oceans, and the atmosphere in a continuous cycle. Heat causes it to evaporate, rising away from the oceans and Earth's surface. In the atmosphere, water molecules cool and bind with miniscule particles (including microorganisms) to form droplets that condense into clouds. Water falls again as precipitation—rain, sleet, or snow—

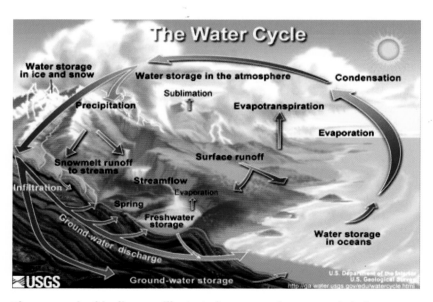

The arrows in this diagram illustrate how water is constantly being redistributed.

A Sea of Garbage

Midway Atoll is like a brilliant white speck in the middle of the Pacific Ocean. The top of an ancient volcano that rises from the deep seafloor, the island has a land surface of only 1,535 acres (621 ha). Used as a U.S. naval base during World War II, in 1998 it became part of the U.S. National Wildlife Refuge system. Today, Midway is home to millions of breeding seabirds. Rare Hawaiian monk seals, green sea turtles, and dolphins shelter in its lagoon, and the surrounding reefs host a wide variety of fishes and marine invertebrates.

Wildlife managers keep a close eye on these populations. Among the issues they did not expect to face was a continuous stream of trash—more than 100 pounds (45 kilograms) per week washes up on the beaches. Located approximately 1,250 miles (2,010 km) northwest of Honolulu, Midway is one of the most isolated islands in the world. What is the source of all this garbage?

Some is dumped directly into the ocean by ships. Much of the trash is carried into the sea by flowing rivers, which pick up anything in their path after heavy rains. Trash is carried along on ocean currents and becomes trapped as those currents circle regions of the globe.

Plastic is the most common component of these "garbage patches." Plastic takes hundreds of years or more to break down and therefore accumulates in the ocean. Pieces may float, but they also mix into the water column, occurring far below the surface. In 2004 biologists found a dead albatross and examined the contents of its stomach. Among other items was a piece of plastic from an

airplane that flew in World War II, dated to 1944. Albatrosses nesting on Midway mistake plastic for food that they would naturally scavenge off the surface of the sea. Seals and turtles become entangled in plastic bags and fishing wire.

Volunteers who clean up trash at Midway Atoll have a few recommendations to improve the situation:

- Dispose of plastic materials properly.
- Reduce, reuse, recycle! Find out about recycling plastics in your area.
- Be a wise consumer—pay attention to your use of and need for disposable products and their fate.

that either winds up in the oceans or soaks into the soil. Plants absorb some water near the surface of the soil; more trickles down to become groundwater. Groundwater may be trapped for centuries. It can either be released at springs, where water-bearing rocks are exposed, or pumped up in wells.

Nitrogen, sulfur, and phosphorus are essential nutrients used to build proteins in the body. Most organisms can't use the nitrogen gas that is so common in the atmosphere. Nitrogen is converted, or fixed, either by lightning or by the action of specific bacteria that live in soil and water. Nitrogen-fixing bacteria convert nitrogen gas to nitrates and ammonia, which can be absorbed by plants. Some of these bacteria live in close association with plant roots, so the nitrogen products can be quickly absorbed. Consumers obtain nitrogen in their food. During decomposition, denitrifying bacteria reverse the process and return nitrogen gas to the atmosphere.

Sulfur comes from rocks, which are gradually broken down by wind and rain. As weathered rock particles become part of the soil, plants are able to absorb their sulfur. It is passed along the food chain and recycled during decomposition. Volcanic activity can also release sulfur into the atmosphere. It may fall in ash or combine with water, returning to ecosystems through the water cycle.

In addition to its role in protein synthesis, phosphorus is also crucial during photosynthesis and respiration as part of the ATP molecule that carries energy. Phosphorus is released only during the weathering of rocks. It does not have a gaseous form; so the phosphorous cycle is limited to rocks and soil, living things, and water. Phosphorus is the Goldilocks of nutrients: ecosystems need amounts that are "just right." A little bit helps plants grow well, shortages make them die off, and an excess may cause overgrowth.

The effects of nutrient pollution can be seen in most populated regions, including Moss Beach. As the community above the tide pools grows, there are more roads, parking lots, and rooftops. These impervious surfaces do not allow rainwater to soak into the ground. Instead, the water runs off quickly into local streams. Chemical pollutants deposited on these impervious surfaces are carried along. Runoff water also gathers fertilizers from local farm fields. Nutrients from runoff can cause the overgrowth of microscopic algae, some of which produce toxic chemicals. Large blooms of algae kill fish. Shellfish such as mussels and clams, which filter the water in search of food, collect toxins in their bodies. People who collect and eat these shellfish are at risk of illness.

The flow of energy and cycling of nutrients began in the earliest archaean ecosystems approximately 3.5 billion years ago. If they remain healthy, these processes can continue to balance and regulate ecosystems, creating a livable planet for millions of species.

Four
Ecosystem Interactions

In the cold waters of the North Pacific Ocean, large pods of orca whales work together to hunt seals. Gray wolf packs team up in the woodlands of Minnesota to chase down deer and moose. On the fringes of a city, a lone peregrine falcon circles high in the sky and then plummets down, reaching a speed of 200 miles per hour (320 km/h) as it dive-bombs an unsuspecting pigeon. By comparison, a garden seems like a peaceful place. But there's plenty of predator-prey action here, too. Every living thing eats or is eaten, a fact that leads to some amazing adaptations.

Eat or Be Eaten

Monarch butterflies are among the most charming animals in the garden. Monarchs have bold, black-and-orange-marked wings and spend their days flitting between flowers. Adult monarchs drink nectar from many species of flowering plants, but when it comes time to lay eggs, the female is very picky. She will place them only on milkweed plants. Monarch eggs are tiny, football shaped, and nearly transparent. The caterpillars are so small upon hatching that they could hide under a grain of rice. Yet carnivores such as spiders, stinkbugs, and wasps manage to find and eat 90 percent of monarch caterpillars. The survivors carry on, nibbling away at milkweed leaves and growing fatter every day.

Milkweed plants make sticky latex, which is the plant's own defense against herbivore predators. Latex contains chemicals called cardiac glycosides that are toxic to most animals. Monarchs have become immune to this toxin. In fact, the milkweed plant is the only food these caterpillars can eat. They store the glycosides and, as they grow, become increasingly more toxic to predators. After the monarch caterpillar metamorphoses into an adult butterfly, it remains toxic. Naïve young birds sometimes eat a monarch, but they soon regret the choice. The butterfly's borrowed toxins aren't deadly, but they cause the bird to become very ill. The bird remembers the monarch's bold coloration and thereafter avoids similar butterflies. Although one butterfly may die to teach this lesson, the larger population benefits.

Although the word "predator" is often applied to interactions between animals, most ecologists consider herbivores to be a special group of parasites or predators. Some animals are adapted for consuming plants, and plants have many ingenious defenses to prevent being eaten. The milkweed plant is a clear example—its cardiac glycosides are strong enough to kill many insect herbivores, and the latex goo in which the chemicals are released is enough to gum up the jaws of even monarch caterpillars. The thorns on a rose stem are another type of deterrent to predators.

While you're in the garden, take a close look at a rabbit as it hops across the grass. The rabbit's brown fur provides camouflage coloration so that it blends in when hiding under bushes. Its long ears give the rabbit an excellent sense of hearing. Notice how the rabbit's eyes are placed on either side of its head. This common adaptation in prey animals gives them peripheral vision. The rabbit can see in a wide arc and will notice if anything is moving—even behind its back. Strong hind legs allow the rabbit to make great leaps into the air and to run quickly when necessary. An owl also has brown coloration.

Its feathers blend in with tree bark, allowing the bird to sit on a branch even in daylight without being noticed. The owl's ears are not visible, but they are as unique as the rabbit's. The ear openings are asymmetrical—one is larger than the other, and they are placed at different heights on the skull—allowing the owl to discern the direction from which sounds are coming. Owl eyes are placed at the front of the face. Because the eyes work together, the owl sees in three dimensions and has depth perception. That's an excellent advantage when gauging the distance of moving prey. The owl's wings are rounded with soft edges. As the bird drops from a perch toward its prey, it flaps as little as possible to make a silent approach. Its talons are fierce weapons, but the rabbit is nimble in its attempts at escape. It's never clear which animal will win this match.

In some cases, camouflage is so complex that the animal actually looks like objects in its environment. The world outside the garden holds many examples. Camouflage may be behavioral, as with a sea anemone that places broken bits of rock and shell over its body. More often camouflage is physiological. An octopus can rapidly change color to match its background. These changes take place in chromatophore cells under the octopus's skin, which contain various colorful pigments. When these cells are stretched, their colors become bold and bright. Platelike structures under the chromatophores, called iridophores, reflect light from the environment to create additional colors and patterns. Walking stick insects are difficult to distinguish from twigs on the forest floor; their relatives, the leaf insects, have wings that mimic leaves.

Praying mantises also have sophisticated forms of camouflage, but the camouflage is no use at night. Insect-eating bats can't see in color, and most rely more on echolocation than vision to find their prey. A bat sends out pulses of sound, which strike any object in its path. The bat listens for echoes, which sound different on the basis of the size, shape, and movement of the object the pulses hit. A mosquito or beetle is no match for a bat, which can "see" the insect using echolocation. The bat is agile and quick, using sound to track the prey until it makes a capture. Praying mantises are another matter.

The Caribbean reef octopus changes its colors and texture to match its surroundings.

These insects have ears. They listen for the high-pitched calls of bats, and when the calls come too close for comfort, praying mantises begin evasive maneuvers. They turn in spirals, dive straight down, or fly hard to one side. These sudden changes in flight path are sometimes enough to confuse a bat, giving the insects a chance to escape.

Predator avoidance also involves communication. Meerkats are slender mammals in the mongoose family. They are found only in the Kalahari Desert of southwestern Africa. Like prairie dogs in North America, meerkats dig complex tunnel systems and live in large communities. Some members of the populations stand as sentries near the burrows and with groups that are feeding farther away. The sentry gives a warning call when it spots a predator. These warning calls distinguish between predators coming from the ground and those that fly. The calls also clarify the threat level by providing information about the distance of the predator. Colony members bolt to their burrows or keep a watchful eye on the predator, depending on the level of immediate risk.

I Need You!

Within communities, populations sometimes develop long-term relationships. These symbiotic interactions last because at least one species benefits.

Divers on tropical coral reefs sometimes report seeing long lines of fish along the seafloor. The fish are often of different species and may even include major predators such as barracuda and groupers. When its turn comes, the fish at the front of the line opens its mouth and waits. A much smaller fish or shrimp swims into its mouth and begins to move around those big, sharp teeth and pick out pieces of food stuck between them. This symbiosis is a mutualism, an association that benefits both animals. The smaller partner obtains a free meal, and the larger fish has a reduced risk of dental decay that could cause infection and death. In mutualism each partner can live without the other—but the relationship makes life better for both.

Mutualisms sometimes go to extremes, as when one partner relies on the other for its survival. This is the case with termites and the protozoa that live in their intestines. Termites eat wood,

A symbiotic relationship exists between cleaner shrimp and larger fish, such as this coral grouper, whose teeth they clean.

but they cannot digest it. The protozoa do this work and thus provide enough nutrients for themselves and their hosts.

Pollination syndromes are another common form of mutualism. These are relationships between pollinators and the plants they visit. They may be so long-standing that the partners have adapted to each other. One example can be found among nectar-feeding bats. They have evolved longer faces as well as extremely long tongues to reach deep into flowers. Bat-pollinated flowers such as saguaro cactus and agave are light-colored, making them visible at night. They also have large, bell-shaped flowers with lots of nectar to attract the bats. Many of these syndromes are economically important, as they guarantee the pollination of foods eaten by humans.

In a commensal relationship, one partner benefits while the other is unaffected. Commensalisms can be hard to define; it's easier to prove that partners are affected than to be sure that they are not. But the remora is often used as an example. The remora is a thin fish with an odd, oval sucker-disk on the top of its head. The remora swims beneath a shark, whale, or sea turtle and attaches to the larger animal's belly using the sucker-disk. There's no apparent benefit or harm to the host, but the remora gets a free ride, and when its host eats, the remora detaches and swims out to grab tidbits from the water. Cattle egrets provide another likely example of commensalism. These long-legged birds wander in the fields among cattle. Insects jump out of the way as cattle walk, and the egrets are there to catch them.

Parasites harm their hosts by feeding on them. Ideally, a parasite does not kill its host because then it loses a food source. Ticks, leeches, and mosquitoes take this strategy. They feed on a host only briefly and live elsewhere. Mistletoe is a plant that attaches to trees. By sinking its roots into a branch, the plant obtains nutrients and water from the host. Both plants can live with this arrangement. Parasites that kill their hosts are usually microorganisms. *Plasmodium* is an extremely common protoctist that can live in human blood. When an *Anopheles* mosquito bites an infected person, it takes in a small amount of blood. The parasite reproduces in the

mosquito's body and is later transmitted to another person. Infection by the *Plasmodium* parasite causes malaria, which is a significant cause of illness and death in tropical countries, especially among children.

Fish biologists are keeping a worried eye on salmon populations, which show increased evidence of infection by sea lice. These shrimplike creatures, less than three-quarters of an inch (2 centimeters) in length, seem particularly common in salmon farms. Farmed salmon live closer together than they would in the wild, and thus, the lice spread easily. Because the salmon are also under more stress, the immune system's ability to fight parasites is reduced. Farms are usually located on the same rivers along which young salmon migrate toward the sea. As the fish swim past, they are exposed to sea lice. Researchers found that young salmon infected with sea lice had only a 5- to 11-percent chance of survival compared with uninfected individuals.

The Changing Seasons

Populations interact with their physical environment as well as with each other. Seasonal change, in particular, produces a wide spectrum of adaptations. A glance out the window in autumn confirms this. Migratory birds are delightful signs of the season—long skeins of geese passing overhead, flitting songbirds among the bushes, and flocks of waterfowl in pools of open water are common in many regions. The summer-green leaves of deciduous trees also respond to the season by painting the autumn landscape in hues of yellow, orange, and red.

Migration has always been a mysterious phenomenon. Birds leave our backyards and disappear. People in other regions see these species a few days or weeks later, but what happened in the time in between? Some of these mysteries are being solved by research conducted by scientists and citizens. In New York City, birders keep a close eye out for migratory birds. On an autumn night you can visit the observation deck atop the Empire State Building, 1,050 feet (320 m) above the bustling city. You'll find a crowd of people there, binoculars pressed to their eyes. They're not looking at the city lights but are gazing skyward in search of the silhouettes of passing birds. At least a hundred migratory bird species have been identified in New York City, and many fly at night to avoid predators. Ecologist Robert DeCandido, who organizes surveys atop the Big Apple's tallest building, reported that more than 19,000 nighttime migrants were spotted during the autumn of 2005.

In late July there are still plenty of worms and clams available along the shorelines where bar-tailed godwits breed in Alaska. But something tells these long-legged, long-billed shorebirds that it's time to go. The godwits spend a couple of weeks eating extra portions to build up a layer of fat around their bodies. Then they are off. A few years ago no one had any idea what route the godwits took between Alaska and their wintering grounds in New Zealand. That information came by chance, when biologists attached small radio transmitters

When the seasons change, godwits fly a nonstop 7,300 miles (11,750 km) from Alaska to New Zealand.

53

On the Wing

Migratory birds face increasing challenges as they move across long distances. Unlike the godwit, many birds must stop on their migratory paths. They need protected areas and sources of food and water. Forests, grasslands, and wetlands have been the traditional migratory stopover sites of North American migratory birds. According to the U.S. Fish and Wildlife Service, these habitats are declining.

- More than 85 percent of forest habitats have been permanently destroyed or logged in the United States.
- Ninety-five percent of tallgrass prairies have been permanently destroyed or converted to agriculture.
- More than 50 percent of all wetlands in the contiguous United States have been drained or filled since the time of European settlement.

The protection of bird habitat benefits humans as well as ecosystems.

- Spruce budworms cause millions of dollars in damage each year in northern and western forests, but five out of every six budworms are eaten by migratory birds.
- Agricultural areas, such as orchards, with woodland nearby usually have more birds than areas without forest, and birds have been shown to consume 95 percent of the tree-damaging moths in those orchards.
- Many tropical birds, as well as birds that migrate to the tropics during the winter, are important for the pollination of numerous valuable species of flowers and trees.

to a few of the birds in New Zealand. Most of the batteries died out after a few weeks, but one lasted for months. What they learned was quite a surprise. Many migratory birds stop at one place or another while migrating to rest and replenish the fat that is quickly burned by flying. Alaska's bar-tailed godwits head straight for New Zealand. The journey takes them across the open waters of the Pacific Ocean, covering 7,300 miles (11,750 km) in just eight days. It is the longest-known nonstop migratory flight of any bird.

An animal's response to winter depends, in part, on how it maintains body temperature. Every organism needs to maintain a fairly constant internal temperature in order to metabolize food. One solution is ectothermy—using the environment to provide heat. Invertebrates, as well as many reptiles and fish, are ectothermic. In order to stay warm, they alter their behavior, finding sunny patches in which to bask and taking long rest breaks to conserve energy.

Endotherms maintain a constant body temperature regardless of conditions in the surrounding environment. Endothermy requires trade-offs—more food or less activity. Desert animals may hide underground all day; their metabolism slows down in a process called torpor. Torpor is not the same as sleep because the animal's body temperature falls below the normal level. Hummingbirds are small birds with an extremely high metabolic rate. These birds use torpor every day, even in mild climates. Hummingbirds migrate in winter, but some other endotherms instead choose hibernation, a long-term torpor in which body temperature, heart rate, and respiration slow dramatically. Hibernating animals must build up large stores of fat, for this is their only energy source during the months of inactivity.

Hibernating bats can survive temperatures as low as 35.6°F (2°C). They may remain in hibernation for many months or awaken during periodic warm spells to find water. As temperatures begin to warm in early spring, bats rouse and begin to seek food. Under normal circumstances it takes a bat about half an hour to wake from hibernation. During this time its heart rate and respiration increase steadily. Blood-flow through

The ectothermic iguana relies on its environment for warmth.

a large fat deposit on the shoulders and back (known as brown adipose tissue, or BAT) helps to warm the animal's blood. This tissue has high concentrations of cellular organelles called mitochondria, which convert food to energy. Mitochondria break down brown fat and create a great deal of heat very quickly. Researchers have found that when bats are roused suddenly from hibernation (such as when humans enter a hibernation cave), they burn BAT at a dramatically faster rate. A single disturbance may use up as much as 80 to 90 percent of a bat's total stored energy for hibernation, compromising its ability to survive the winter.

Like animals, plants respond to changes in the availability of resources. The most important change is a reduction in sunlight. Earth takes a year to make one complete revolution around the sun. Throughout this period Earth also rotates on its own axis. But because Earth is tilted on its axis, for part of the year the Southern Hemisphere (south of the equator) is exposed directly to the sun while the Northern Hemisphere is angled away. At this time it is winter in the Northern Hemisphere. Half a year later, when Earth reaches the far side of its orbit, the Northern Hemisphere gets more light and experiences summer. During winter, plants may not have enough light to perform photosynthesis. In some areas they may also have to deal with freezing temperatures. Plants respond in different ways to these challenges. Annual plants live only one year. They die off in autumn but leave seeds in the soil to start a new population the following spring. Perennial plants live for more than one year. In cold climates their aboveground stems and leaves may wither, but their roots and underground parts such as tubers remain alive in a dormant state. No growth takes place during dormancy, but the plant can resume its normal activity when conditions allow. Dormancy is also useful for desert and grassland plants. They become inactive during times of extreme heat and drought and can quickly begin to grow after a rain.

Trees exhibit different responses to winter conditions. Coniferous trees such as pines and firs produce seeds in cones and have needlelike leaves. Conifers often grow in regions where winter is long and there is only a short period for growth.

In winter they may stop growing, but conifers never enter a true state of dormancy. The trees remain green and lush year-round, even when a heavy layer of snow covers the ground. This state allows them to take advantage of any day that is warm and bright enough to allow photosynthesis. By contrast, many deciduous trees lose their leaves in autumn and regrow them in spring. Trees lose a lot of water from their leaves. In winter, if the ground is frozen, the trees cannot replenish their water supply. Dropping their leaves reduces water loss at a time when there's not much opportunity to photosynthesize anyway. Winter may seem like a desolate season. It's merely a break in the usual busyness of life, which bursts forth again at the first opportunity.

Seasonal events such as leaf growth, flowering, ripening of fruits, animal migration, and reproduction are related to

A 2006 study of Europe's plants and fruiting vegetation revealed that fruit-bearing plants ripened earlier than they did in the prior decade.

temperature as well as changes in day length. According to the National Aeronautics and Space Agency (NASA), global temperatures have increased 0.7 to 1.4 °F (0.4 to 0.8 °C) since the late 1800s. (The amount of change varies by region.) A 2006 study of more than 560 European plant and animal species revealed that 78 percent of the plants were leafing, flowering, and fruiting as much as 2.5 days earlier than they had a decade before. Climate change threatens to alter many of the seasonal patterns we have come to take for granted.

Five
A Changing World

Nicolaus Steno was neither a great explorer nor a highly trained scientist. He was simply a curious young physician from Denmark who had an interest in nature and geology. Steno was particularly curious about fossils. In the mid–1600s, when Steno was born, most people assumed that fossils grew inside of rocks. This idea made no sense to him. Steno knew that tree roots grew underground. They became gnarled from twisting around hard objects that blocked their path in the soil. But fossils had consistent shapes. If they grew underground, why weren't they misshapen like roots? Steno was also bothered by the apparent lack of purpose for fossils. He wondered why God would cause something to grow if it had no use. Steno's ideas developed as he examined a set of hard, triangular objects that were common in rock layers and on beaches near his adopted home in Florence, Italy. Local people called them "tongue stones." Steno had already dissected the head of a dead great white shark and seen its teeth. He concluded that tongue stones were fossilized sharks' teeth. This presented an intriguing possibility. Could all fossils be parts of living things?

Steno then began to look at the formation of sedimentary rocks. These rocks consist of particles eroded from older rocks. They often contain layers of different sediments—and different fossils. Steno said that when sediments are mixed in a fluid, they settle at the bottom of lakes and oceans. Over time, heat and pressure compress the sediments into horizontal layers. Anything solid that is trapped within the sediments will also become part of the rock layer—including the bodies of dead animals. This, he said, explains how fossils become embedded in rock. Steno also reasoned that in any sequence of rock layers, the oldest are always at the bottom.

Steno's principles were widely accepted. But many questions remained about Earth's geology. Why do rock layers remain flat in some places, yet elsewhere they are contorted and broken? Why are there canyons here and mountains there? Geologists began to realize that rock layers are sometimes changed after being laid down. Some suggested that rare but catastrophic events, such as earthquakes, are responsible for these changes. In the 1790s James Hutton disputed this idea. He proposed that gradual processes transform Earth's surface rather than periodic, dramatic forces that wreak rapid change. A few decades later geologist Charles Lyell traveled throughout Europe and North America. He found a great deal of evidence supporting Hutton's idea. The most obvious was erosion, the incremental wearing down of rock by wind, rain, ice, and other forces. Lyell called this slow process uniformitarianism. On the basis of the amount of erosion he saw, Lyell concluded that Earth must be very old.

In 1815 William Smith used Steno's geological principles to explain how fossils reveal the evolutionary time line of life. Smith's work as a canal engineer gave him many opportunities to observe rocks around Britain. He noticed that certain fossils always occurred together, even in different parts of the British countryside. Moreover, fossil groups did not occur in random places—they were in the same rock layers from place to place. Smith remembered what Steno had said: new sedimentary layers form atop old layers. Therefore, reasoned Smith, fossils in the uppermost layers must be more recent than those below.

The Voyage of Charles Darwin

Charles Darwin left England aboard the HMS *Beagle* in 1831, a young man with the urge to escape his fate. Darwin's father wanted him to be a doctor. When he showed no interest in this family profession, the boy was sent to Cambridge University for training in the ministry. At heart, though, Darwin had always been drawn to nature. When the opportunity arose to travel the world as assistant naturalist on the *Beagle*, Darwin convinced his father to let him go. The journey, which had been planned to last for two years, stretched to five. Darwin eventually took over as lead naturalist. He collected specimens of plants and animals everywhere the ship stopped and made detailed observations in his notebooks.

Darwin was not familiar with the work of William Smith. But he had brought along several books that described uniformitarianism, including Charles Lyell's *Principles of Geology*. Darwin saw evidence from around the world that supported Lyell's thinking, such as seashells embedded in rocks at the highest point of the Andes Mountains in South America.

Charles Darwin took extensive notes on the plants and creatures he encountered on his travels.

When the *Beagle* stopped at Punta Alta, Argentina, in August 1833, he explored local beaches and found fossils of strange and amazing animals in the cliffs. A giant shell resembled those he had seen on armadillos but was many times larger. He found one fossil that was the size of an elephant but had teeth for gnawing, like a rodent's. He recognized a slothlike animal among the fossils, but it was as big as an elephant— many times larger than living sloths. Darwin had never seen or heard of such creatures. He began to suspect that these fossils represented animals that no longer lived on Earth.

Darwin had not only read Lyell's ideas about the changes on Earth's surface but also studied ideas about evolution. It was not a popular idea, but some scientists had previously suggested that organisms on Earth could change over time. Fossils were one piece of evidence. Another clue came from the distribution of living things. Darwin noticed that some species were common and widespread across the continents, while others were found only in one place. These patterns did not seem to be random. Years later he would write, "the naturalist in travelling, for instance, from north to south never fails to be struck by the manner in which successive groups of beings, specifically distinct, yet clearly related, replace each other."

In 1836 Darwin returned to England with a large collection of biological specimens and many new ideas. Of particular interest to him were a group of finches he had found on the Galápagos Islands, a chain of thirteen volcanic islands and more than a hundred rocky islets off the western coast of South America. Although many of the finches were similar in appearance, one consistent difference intrigued him: each had a different sort of beak. Some beaks were long and narrow; others were short and sharp or thick like those of parrots. Darwin believed that beak shape was an adaptation for feeding.

Darwin noted the resemblance of these finches to those he saw in South America, more than 500 miles (800 km) away. He developed an explanation for their similarities and differences. At some point in the past, he said, a group of South American finches must have reached the islands—perhaps in a storm or just by flying. Over time, populations spread across

1. Geospiza magnirostris.
3. Geospiza parvula.
2. Geospiza fortis.
4. Certhidea olivasea.

Darwin's study of finches from the Galápagos Islands contributed to this theory of evolution.

the islands into habitats with different resources. Adaptations in beak shapes allowed these populations to feed on a variety of foods—large nuts, small seeds, insects, and so forth. In his book *The Voyage of the Beagle*, Darwin wrote, "seeing this gradation and diversity of structure in one small, intimately related group of birds, one might really fancy that from an original paucity of birds in this archipelago, one species had been taken and modified for different ends."

Darwin suggested that something in nature and in organisms influenced the way evolution took place. He called this process natural selection. The idea was elegant in its simplicity. Individuals have traits that help them survive. But in any population, individuals exhibit varying forms of the same trait. For example, one fox might have thick fur while another's is thinner. If the environment is cool, the fox with thick fur is more likely to survive and reproduce. The trait for thick fur is passed to its offspring (along with many other traits). If the

environment remains cool, the thick-fur trait will begin to dominate. The accumulation of many new traits over a long period of time causes speciation—the formation of a new species that cannot breed with populations of the old species.

It was a dangerous career move to publish anything about evolution. Darwin spent two decades pondering and fine-tuning his idea, unwilling to take the risk. In the 1850s a young British naturalist pushed Darwin into action. During his travels through the tropics of Asia and South America, Alfred Russel Wallace made extensive observations of the effect of geography on the distribution of species. He became convinced that traits are passed through populations and are driven by a force he called "survival of the fittest." The men were now competitors to publish the most innovative and disputed idea of their time. In 1858 they agreed to make a presentation together on natural selection to the Linnaean Society of London. A year later Darwin's *The Origin of Species* was published.

How Does Evolution Happen?

North America's Chihuahuan Desert spreads across more than 175,000 square miles (453,250 km²) in northern Mexico and the southwestern United States. The Chihuahuan receives less than 10 inches (25 cm) of precipitation per year and is prone to rapid changes in temperature—days can be scorchingly hot, while nighttime temperatures can plunge. You might find it hard to tell this desert from the Sonoran Desert that borders it to the west, but plants provide a good clue. Cacti of varying shapes and sizes dominate the Sonoran Desert. In the Chihuahuan you'll find bushy mesquite and creosote plants with waxy leaves, which reduce water loss, and long taproots to reach water deep beneath the surface. Agave and lechugilla are succulent plants that store water in their leaves. Sharp spines along the leaf edges deter predators from munching. Mammals, such as the kangaroo rat, get almost all of their water from the food they eat, rather than by drinking.

Within this larger desert is a unique ecosystem called White Sands. In 1933 the U.S. National Park Service set aside

Passing It On

Darwin understood that adaptations are inherited but could not identify a mechanism for the process. An Austrian monk named Gregor Mendel answered this question with a series of simple experiments in the 1860s. Mendel worked with pea plants from the garden. He noticed that they had pairs of contrasting traits: yellow or green seeds, wrinkled or smooth seeds, and so forth. Mendel started with plants that were "true breeding"—they self-pollinated and produced offspring that looked like themselves. Then he began to cross plants, testing for one trait at a time. When he crossed true-breeding plants with green seeds and those with yellow seeds, plants in the next generation all had yellow seeds. The next step was to cross these plants. Their offspring had yellow and green seeds in a ratio of three to one. This same pattern appeared for all of the seven traits Mendel examined. He concluded that each parent contributes a "factor" for a trait. Some factors, he said, can mask others. The appearance of a trait in offspring depends on the combination of factors they inherit.

Today we know that the nucleus of each cell contains double-stranded molecules called DNA (deoxyribonucleic acid). These contain genetic information and are able to replicate themselves when cells divide, so each new cell gets an exact replica. Genes are regions on DNA that code for particular characteristics, and it is these that are affected by natural selection. Evolution also occurs as a result of mutations (random changes) that produce novel traits. Mutations are comparatively rare events but are significant because they provide the variation in populations upon which natural selection can act.

this little desert-within-a-desert to protect 275 square miles (712 km²) of white sand dunes, the largest of their kind in the world. The white dunes, made of a mineral called gypsum, are the remnants of a shallow sea that covered this region more than 250 million years ago. This sea had high concentrations of sulfur and calcium. As the water dried up, gypsum crystals were left behind. About 70 million years ago the whole region was pushed upward by the collision of two of Earth's large landmasses (called plates) along the western edge of the continent. The center of this uplifted dome began to drop 10 million years ago, forming a deep valley completely surrounded by mountains.

For millions of years, rainwater has swept down the mountain slopes, eroding the soft gypsum and depositing it on the valley floor. Until the last ice age ended, about ten thousand years ago, these minerals sat at the bottom of a lake. Since then a warming climate has gradually evaporated the lake. The exposed crystals gradually eroded, forming sand that blows from west to east through the valley. The dunes undulate and shift with the daily and seasonal winds. A single dune may move as much as 30 feet (9 m) in a year.

Animals at White Sands are similar to those in the Chihuahuan Desert at large. But they show some interesting adaptations. Whiptail lizards are usually boldly colorful, with tails, heads, and feet tinted in brilliant turquoise and bold stripes down the back. At White Sands these same lizards have beige, stripeless backs, and their blue marks are muted. Lesser earless lizards are typically brown with an obvious pattern of orange spots. Not so at White Sands, where these lizards look like they've been dipped in white ashes. Deer mice have also changed color at White Sands. Their forest-dwelling relatives are brown with gray bellies; dune mice are white-bellied with beige backs.

What's the point behind all this change? Imagine how obvious bright-colored lizards and mice must look against the colorless background of the white dunes. An animal's chance of survival is severely compromised when it is so exposed. Predators have a harder time spotting pale-colored individuals.

In order to survive, organisms have adapted to their environment. For example, the earless lizard in Arizona is brown and orange (top). However, in the White Sands Desert, it is pale and blends into its natural habitat (bottom).

69

These three species, and probably others that have not yet been discovered, have adapted to the conditions at White Sands.

At this point darker-colored lizards can still mate with lighter ones, and the same is true with deer mice. But that is likely to change. A study conducted at New Mexico State University showed that light-colored, male earless lizards chose mates with similar light coloration. This means they are unlikely to interbreed with darker lizards from the regions surrounding White Sands. A single adaptation is not enough to cause speciation. But lack of breeding between the populations will cause increasing numbers of differences between them— especially if each population continues to develop new adaptations. Eventually, White Sands populations may develop into new species.

Evolution happens as the result of isolation. Pale species at White Sands National Monument and Darwin's Galápagos finches represent two distinct types of isolation that can lead to speciation. At White Sands there is no physical barrier to prevent pale lizards and mice from breeding with nearby populations that live on darker rocks and sand. But the two populations are each specialized in their own foods, nesting sites, and so on. Their niches are just different enough that they don't often meet. Lizards and mice at White Sands naturally breed with individuals in their own community. And because light-colored individuals are more likely to survive in that community, that trend, called sympatric speciation, has been favored by natural selection.

Allopatric speciation occurs when a small population becomes geographically isolated from the main population. Natural selection acts on traits that adapt the small population to its new setting. Over time, the small population accumulates so many adaptations that it is no longer able to interbreed with the original population. It is a new species. Allopatric speciation is common on island chains, as in the Galápagos. It also takes place when major geologic disruptions, such as earthquakes and volcanic eruptions, divide populations in the same landscape.

Ecosystem Change

Species evolve in response to changes in their environment. Likewise, ecosystems usually remain fairly stable unless they are disturbed. Disturbances may be abiotic or biotic. A major windstorm that sweeps through a forest can knock down hundreds of trees in a single afternoon. Suddenly the understory and floor of the forest are flooded with light. Certain plants in the community die off because they cannot tolerate this much exposure. Others thrive and begin to spread. The end result might be the same if a parasite invaded the tallest trees and killed them off. Whatever the cause, ecosystem change as the result of disturbance is called succession.

Over the past three decades the citizens of central Washington State have been able to observe succession firsthand. With an altitude of 9,677 feet (2,950 m) at its summit, Mount St. Helens was not the largest of the Cascade Mountains, but it was one of the most picturesque. Like the mountains you learned to draw as a child, Mount St. Helens was shaped like an upside-down V with a cap of snow and symmetrically sloping sides. In March 1980 earthquakes began to rattle the volcano and surrounding regions. Thousands of these tremors shook the region over the next two months. News stations across the United States turned their attention to this rural area, which many Americans had never before noticed. Would the volcano soon erupt, asked eager newscasters, or was this just a rumbling portent of future disaster? An explosion seemed increasingly likely to geologists and locals who watched the mountain's northern rim begin to protrude and swell. Their answer came on the morning of May 18. At 8:32 a.m., Mount St. Helens shuddered as another earthquake rippled under its surface. The upper northern wall of the volcano broke free and crumpled toward the river valley below. Almost instantly, 1,312 feet (400 m) of the mountaintop had been shaved off.

A blast of rock, ice, and searing steam followed the initial landslide, roaring down the northern face of the volcano and

Change Goes Both Ways

Life on Earth has been evolving for billions of years. Extinction is the other side of change. Extinction may occur almost invisibly as species adapt and change over generations. But life on Earth has also been marked by several massive extinction events. During each, great percentages of Earth's species have been lost. In the wake of extinction, new groups evolve under altered environmental conditions.

- The first known mass extinction occurred in the Ordovician geological period, about 440 million years ago. Dramatic cooling of the climate caused ice to form on land and the sea level to fall. All life was found in the oceans at that time, which spelled disaster. About 85 percent of species became extinct.

- Fluctuations in sea level led to the Devonian extinctions 365 million years ago. Many types of coral-reef animals were affected, along with some early fish and plant groups. In total, 80 percent of species died out.

- At the end of the Permian period, 250 million years ago, some organisms had moved onto land, and diversity was at its peak. Many causes contributed to this extinction event, including volcanic activity that added climate-altering dust and chemicals to the atmosphere. Life barely survived—about 95 percent of species became extinct.

- In the Triassic period, 200 million years ago, volcanic activity and sea level changes once again affected the planet. The species loss was about 80 percent.

- The most recent mass extinction event took place 65 million years ago, when a large asteroid struck Earth. The Cretaceous period ended with extinction of the dinosaurs and many species in the oceans—75 percent of Earth's biodiversity in all. Mammals survived this event and quickly began to fill the niches once dominated by dinosaurs.

across the landscape at speeds up to 680 miles per hour (1,100 km/h). Ice fields atop Mount St. Helens were instantly melted by the eruption, producing mud that poured down the volcano's southern slopes. A mushroom cloud blossomed overhead and was picked up by winds. Ash rained down around the volcano and was carried far to the east.

Scientists wondered how the blast would affect the formerly lush forest that had grown around Mount St. Helens. It became clear that several levels of damage had been done. Snow cover and hillsides reduced the impact of the blast in some areas. Here plants began to sprout within weeks of the blast. Decomposers set to work on fallen trees, releasing nutrients to further spur new growth. This phenomenon is called secondary succession and occurs where soil remains after a disturbance. Primary succession took place on the sites that had been completely covered by rock rubble, mud, or ash. Even these areas showed growth within a year or two. Hardy lupines, with their cheery lavender flowers, popped up among the rubble wherever wind had deposited the least bit of soil. Their lives and deaths added material to the soil until scattered gardens of sedge grass, penstemons, asters, Indian paintbrushes, and other flowers spread across the mountainside. When ecologists examined the most damaged sites in 2000, they found shrubs and trees among the smaller plants. Red alder and cottonwood trees on the rocks had grown up to 33 feet (10 m) tall. Life carried on in the face of adversity, as it has in so many places throughout Earth's long history.

Expect the Unexpected

Ecosystem change has taken place throughout the history of Earth, but human behavior is now a driving force behind it in many parts of the world. Islands are particularly susceptible to change because they are comparatively small and isolated. In the 1850s ranchers decided that Santa Cruz Island, one of a group of islands just offshore from California's central coast, would make a good place to raise sheep. Ranchers shifted to cattle in the 1930s; many sheep were removed, but a small

Lupines regenerate on the volcanic slopes of Mount St. Helens in Washington State.

population was left to roam wild on the island. Within a few decades they and the cattle had eaten the vegetation down until only bare rock was left.

Santa Cruz Island is jointly owned by the U.S. National Park Service and a nonprofit organization called the Nature Conservancy. Biologists from both organizations agreed to remove all livestock in the late 1980s. Expecting the native vegetation to return, they looked for pine forests and patches of coastal scrub (characterized by thick-growing shrubs such as coyote brush, blackberry, and monkeyflower) to come back to the hillsides. Instead, many parts of the island were blanketed with fennel, a European plant often used in cooking and for treatment of certain ailments in humans and cattle.

It's likely that this plant was introduced into the ranchers' gardens and spread, as many alien species do, into areas where the soil had been disturbed by livestock. Even after removing livestock, fennel remained a dominant plant because it had no native herbivores to reduce its population. Today biologists are working to plant native species on various parts of the island, giving them a fighting chance against the fennel. Similar stories can be told in places around the world.

Six
Everything Has Limits

In the 1830s the British economist Thomas Malthus (1766–1834) observed recent changes in human population and worried. Malthus knew that living things were compelled to reproduce. He wrote,

> In plants and irrational animals, the view of the subject is simple. They are all impelled by a powerful instinct to the increase of their species; and this instinct is interrupted by no doubts about providing for their offspring. Wherever therefore there is liberty, the power of increase is exerted; and the superabundant effects are repressed afterwards by want of room and nourishment.

Malthus pointed out that healthy populations tend to increase exponentially. Two become four; these mate and become eight, and so on. But food growth is limited by space; resources cannot be doubled at that same exponential rate. Eventually a fast-growing population will outstrip its own

food supply. Malthus had been calculating population growth in the United States, which had just received its independence from Britain a few decades before. He used this nation as an example. "In the northern states of America," he noted, ". . . the population has been found to double itself, for above a century and a half successively, in less than twenty-five years."

How Many Is Too Many?

When a population moves into a new environment without competitors, exponential growth is often the result. This was the case in America, where colonists found a comparatively low density of American Indians living on a large area of land. In addition to birthrates, population is affected by death rates and immigration. American Indians were severely affected by diseases brought over by European colonists. Their populations declined dramatically, further reducing competition for land and resources. Early colonists initially suffered high death rates while they adjusted to new diseases and challenges. But more colonists continued to arrive from Europe. Approximately one hundred men established the first permanent English settlement at Jamestown, Virginia, in 1607. By 1775, just before the American Revolution, the population of colonial America had reached almost 2.6 million.

Another important component of population is density; that is, the number of individuals in a given area. Density, which may vary from place to place, can increase or decrease stress on the population. Some species attempt to control a territory by maintaining population density. This is a way of protecting a patch of high-quality resources. Wolf packs have complex behaviors for protecting their territories, including marking the boundaries with urine and howling to intimidate other packs and lone wolves. When it becomes necessary, wolves will fight to protect their space. Certain plants also protect territory. For example, black walnuts and related trees produce a toxic chemical called juglone from their roots. This chemical permeates the soil around the tree. Some plants are not able to grow in the presence of juglone; fewer plants means less competition for the trees.

It's not possible to describe a "perfect" population size, but ecologists sometimes calculate an ecosystem's carrying capacity; that is, the maximum number of individuals that can survive in a system without harming it. If a population begins to exceed its carrying capacity, limiting factors begin to control population size. Limiting factors are shared resources that occur in finite amounts in the environment. When populations are too large, individuals must begin to compete for those resources. Limiting factors typically include food, living space, and nutrients.

The abiotic environment can exert strong and unpredictable effects on population size. The eruption at Mount St. Helens provides a case in point. Populations of many species declined dramatically after the eruption. A volcanic eruption is not related to population size or density, so ecologists label it as a density-independent factor. Floods, fires, droughts, and climate change are also density-independent.

A Long (or Short) Life

If you have pets, you've probably noticed that some types of animals live longer than others. Aquarium fish might survive for a year or two. Larger pets, such as cats and dogs, may be part of your family for ten to twenty years. The same is true in ecosystems, where species come in all different sizes and have radically different life spans. Reproductive strategies are often correlated to size. Remember the monarch butterfly from the garden? Like many insects, it has a short life span—never more than a year and often just a couple of months. By contrast, the bird that eats the monarch may live for several years (depending on the species). Researchers once caught a blue jay that had been fitted with a leg band more than seventeen years before.

Reproductive strategies also relate to niche. Think about the owl and rabbit from the garden. Rabbits produce several litters each year, with several kits (baby rabbits) per litter. Owls nest once a year, usually hatching only two or three owlets. Why the difference in family size? It has to do with the food

chain. Prey animals often have many young, because most of them will be eaten before they reach adulthood.

Populations may also experience wild swings in size called boom-and-bust cycles. This begins with exponential growth in a short-lived species that has access to good resources. A classic example is the lemming, a small rodent species found in the tundra biome around the Arctic. Lemmings live under the snow layer, where they eat grasses and plant roots. They reproduce quickly; their large numbers enable local predator populations to increase as well. Snowy owls and great gray owls in the Arctic depend heavily on lemmings in their diet.

A snowy owl clutches a lemming in its beak. Snowy owls depend on lemmings as a main part of their diet. A depletion in lemmings would adversely affect the owls.

After a few years, however, the large lemming population begins to outstrip its food supply. When this happens, lemmings abandon their homes and head in new directions in search of food. Predators in the old lemming habitat are left hungry. Such events often spur a corresponding southward migration of owls. Birders in the United States can always tell when the Arctic lemming population has gone bust, because owl populations suddenly increase across the northern United States. In the winter of 2004–05, more than 5,200 migratory great gray owls were counted in Minnesota alone.

Share and Share Alike

Just a couple hours' drive south of Moss Beach's fabulous tide pools is another coastal wonder. Elkhorn Slough (pronounced "slew") is an estuary, or coastal wetland, where freshwater from inland mixes with saltwater as the tides rise each day. The slough hosts a wide variety of plants that are adapted to deal with changing concentrations of salt and shifting levels of water.

In a single day you might see thousands of shorebirds at Elkhorn Slough wandering through the shallow water or skittering across the sand and mud. Round bodies and disproportionately long legs and beaks give shorebirds a slightly comical appearance, but don't be fooled. These birds are all business. It's not unusual to see large flocks of a single species or birds of several species foraging near each other on the same small stretch of beach or mudflat. You might wonder whether all of these species are competing for the same resources. It's a reasonable question. Competition occurs both within and between populations. Watch the sanderlings for evidence. These charming little shorebirds stick in tight flocks as they forage. Yet the flock's main purpose isn't to share food—it is to provide many eyes to avoid predators. When feeding, every bird looks after itself. If it spies a tasty sand flea, a sanderling will sprint to grab it before another bird can. And if it finds a spot with a cluster of insects, the sanderling will eat every one it can catch. Birds fight over goodies on the beach and constantly endeavor to find the best for themselves.

Sanderlings feed in flocks. As some feed, others stand sentry for predators.

You'll rarely see a lot of plovers together, but they may be mixed in with sanderlings. The two species are about the same size. Both have slightly elongated bills, which they use to jab repeatedly at the sand and mud. How do these birds avoid competition? It turns out that plovers grab prey off the surface of the beach, while sanderlings hunt for tiny insects, crabs, and worms living in the top layers of sand. The many shorebirds that share this beach are similarly adapted to use different resources. The willet wanders along the wave line or in wet mud probing for shelled prey about 2 inches (5 cm) below the surface. Godwits have even longer legs and walk in the shallow water, plunging their 6-inch (15-cm) bills into the sand in search of worms. Avocets also have rapierlike beaks, but they are not interested in worms. Instead of dipping into the sand and mud, these lanky birds sweep their upcurved bills through the water to stir up and then scoop up small creatures in the water. This partitioning of resources allows many populations to share the resources of a single ecosystem.

The Russian microbiologist Georgii Gause was curious about the effects of competition. He studied two species of *Paramecium* (a type of protoctist) in the laboratory. Both species were kept together, sharing the same space and food. Gause found that one of the species was consistently better at obtaining food. This population grew, while the other eventually failed. He referred to this process as competitive exclusion. When two populations share a very similar niche, Gause said, one will almost always outcompete the other. The weaker population must either move to a new location to obtain the resource, adapt to use a new resource, or die out. *Paramecium* has a short life span, so it was easy for Gause to observe this interaction. In most cases competitive exclusion—like all forms of adaptation—is a slow process that happens over generations.

Living Lightly on the Planet

We humans are the ultimate generalists. We are spread out over almost every part of the planet, and we make use of a wide variety of resources. Over the past century, as our population has grown dramatically and we have developed the ability to transport goods over long distances, we no longer simply take a large proportion of what is in our immediate ecosystem. We obtain stuff from many other ecosystems as well. This puts each of us in competition with other species and with other humans around the world. Ecologists believe that Earth can sustain a large human population—but only if people everywhere reduce their footprint. That means consuming a little less, creating a smaller amount of waste, and making sure that our behaviors enhance natural systems rather than impair them.

In the mid–twentieth century, when ecologists first began to notice damage to the environment, very few laws existed to

Picky Eaters

Competition leads individuals to strive for the highest-quality and greatest proportion of resources in their environment, and that can be stressful. Populations that experience a lot of competition usually find ways to relieve the stress. One approach is to generalize. Rather than depending on one food source, generalists select from many. Honeybees are generalists; they visit many flowers in their local environment to obtain nectar and pollen. American black bears are also generalists. They gather berries, nuts, and honey; scavenge animals they find dead; and occasionally kill small animals, such as fawns.

Specialists focus on one resource. Squash bees feed only on the blossoms of plants in the squash family, which includes pumpkins, zucchini, and butternut squash. These bees don't form large colonies, as honeybees do. Each female digs a nest in the ground in which to raise her larvae, while males sleep inside squash flowers. Another familiar specialist is the giant panda (right). These beautiful black-and-white bears live in the mountains of western China and feed almost exclusively on bamboo.

To reduce competition, the density of specialist populations is often lower in a given ecosystem than that of generalists. Such species are at greater risk of extinction, particularly when habitat loss removes their primary food source.

In 2009 the International Union for Conservation of Nature (IUCN) reported that, of 47,677 well-studied species worldwide, 17,291 were threatened with extinction.

control the use and abuse of natural resources. Aldo Leopold expressed his concerns in *A Sand County Almanac*:

> We abuse the land because we regard it as a commodity belonging to us. When we see land as a community to which we belong, we may begin to use it with love and respect. There is no other way for land to survive the impact of mechanized man, nor for us to reap from it the esthetic harvest it is capable, under science, of contributing to culture.

Two decades later, Senator Gaylord Nelson of Wisconsin worried about the same problems as Leopold. Inspired by mass protests against the Vietnam War, Senator Nelson organized Earth Week as a way to encourage the U.S. government to protect the nation's environmental resources. Americans jumped on the idea. In April 1970, 20 million people around the country participated in demonstrations and clean-up activities.

Ten years later Nelson wrote an article recounting the accomplishments in the years since the first Earth Day. The U.S. government had passed major legislation protecting air, water, and endangered species. Lake Erie, which was so polluted that it caught fire several times in the 1960s, had recovered quickly—just one sign that the environment was responding to these changes. He ended with a reminder that rings as true today as it did then.

> So long as the human species inhabits the Earth, proper management of its resources will be the most fundamental issue we face. Our very survival will depend upon whether or not we are able to preserve, protect and defend our environment. We are not free to decide about whether or not our environment "matters." It does matter, apart from any political exigencies. We disregard the needs of our ecosystem at our mortal peril.

Humans can contribute to protecting and preserving Earth by maintaining its natural resources.

This is a sobering but honest reminder: Environmental damage is a legacy of the modern world. We have a choice to act with or against the ecosystems that sustain us. You don't have to throw away all of your belongings and live in a cabin without running water. The key is to balance what you take with what you give. That's what makes everything work on the living Earth.

Working for the World

You might wonder what one person can do to make a difference. The first step is simply to appreciate your own role in nature. Become familiar with the ecosystem in which you live. Notice problems and point them out to your parents and teachers. Read a newspaper, and then read a different source. Compare the stories you hear with what you see and experience. News is not always free of bias, and it's good to consult a variety of sources before forming opinions. Then see how you can take action in your community. Write your local government officials. Most city governments have environmental task forces that are eager to have young participants.

Citizen science is another great way to get involved. Are you interested in birds, turtles, flowers, or water quality? Many organizations ask for help from the public to collect scientific data. It's a great way to combine time in nature with learning and community service. While you're outside, create some habitat for wildlife. Research the plants that are native to your area, and plant some in your yard. If you don't have a yard, call the local park district and sign up for a planting crew—they always need help. Build birdhouses and bat boxes. The possibilities are endless.

Notes

Chapter One

p. 13, ". . . this trait appeared approximately 5.8 million years ago.": John Pickrell, "Timeline: Human Evolution," September 4, 2006, www.newscientist.com/article/dn9989-timeline-human-evolution.html (accessed May 1, 2010).

p. 14, "In 1800 the world population was . . .": Population Reference Bureau, "Human Population: Teachers' Guide," n.d., www.prb.org/Educators/TeachersGuides/HumanPopulation/PopulationGrowth.aspx (accessed February 23, 2010).

p. 14, "It exceeded 6.8 billion in 2010.": U.S. Census Bureau, "U.S. & World Population Clocks," 2010, www.census.gov/main/www/popclock.html (accessed May 5, 2010).

p. 14, "Together the U.S. and China use 21 percent . . .": ed. Chris Hails, *Living Planet Report 2008* (Gland, Switzerland: WWF International, 2008), pp. 14–15.

p. 14, ". . . may reach nine billion by 2050.": Population Reference Bureau.

p. 16, ". . . rapidly growing demands for food, fresh water . . .": Millennium Ecosystem Assessment Board, "Overview of the Millennium Ecosystem Assessment," 2005, www.maweb.org/en/About.aspx (accessed March 3, 2010).

p. 16, "MEA scientists list five areas of concern . . .": Georgina Mace et al., "Chapter 4: Biodiversity," in *Millennium Ecosystem Assessment: Ecosystems and Human Well-Being—Biodiversity Synthesis* (Washington, DC: Island Press, 2005), www.maweb.org/en/index.aspx (accessed January 23, 2010), pp. 96–99.

p. 18, ". . . *Living Planet Index 2008* adds another risk to the list.": Chris Hails, p. 4.

p. 18, "In 1970, researchers visited California's . . .": Joseph E. Brown, *The Return of the Brown Pelican* (Baton Rouge: Louisiana State University Press, 1983), ch. 5.

p. 18, "For decades DDT was made in a Los Angeles factory" . . .": Center for Biological Diversity, "California Brown Pelican," n.d., www.biologicaldiversity.org/campaigns/esa_works/profile_pages/CaliforniaBrownPelican.html (accessed June 22, 2010).

p. 19, ". . . removed from the Endangered Species List . . .": U.S. Fish and Wildlife Service, "Species Profile for Brown Pelican," June 22, 2010, www.fws.gov/ecos/ajax/speciesProfile/profile/speciesProfile.action?spcode = B02L (accessed June 22, 2010).

p. 19, "In the upper atmosphere ozone forms a thin layer . . .": Brien Sparling, "The Ozone Layer," NASA, www.nas.nasa.gov/About/Education/Ozone/ozonelayer.html (accessed June 20, 2010).

p. 20, "In the 1980s it was discovered that the ozone . . .": U.S. Environmental Protection Agency, "Montreal Protocol One-Page Fact Sheet," n.d., www.epa.gov/

ozone/downloads/MP20_FactSheet.pdf (accessed June 20, 2010).

p. 20, "When we try to pick out anything by itself . . .": John Muir, *My First Summer in the Sierra*, in *Nature Writings* (New York: Library of America, 1992), p. 245.

Chapter Two

p. 21, "Biologists have so far described and named . . .": Georgina Mace et al., p. 88.

p. 25, ". . . just one-fourth the size of New York's Manhattan . . .": "History of Smithsonian Tropical Research Institute," n.d., www.stri.org/english/about_stri/history.php (accessed March 13, 2010).

p. 25, "Although tropical rain forest are found on only 7 percent . . .": Brian Groombridge and Martin D. Jenkins, *World Atlas of Biodiversity* (Berkeley: University of California Press, 2002), p. 79.

p. 25, "Yet a 2008 survey found more than 1,200 species . . .": David K. A. Barnes et al., "Marine, intertidal, freshwater and terrestrial biodiversity of an isolated polar archipelago," *Journal of Biogeography*, November 24, 2008, pp. 756–769.

p. 26, ". . . pollen, algae, and bacteria are common . . .": Sarah Everts, "Bacteria in Clouds," *Chemical & Engineering News*, April 14, 2008, http://pubs.acs.org/cen/science/86/8615sci1.html (accessed January 12, 2010).

p. 27, "Bacteria have also been discovered in tiny puddles . . .": Debora MacKenzie, "Gold mine holds life untouched by the sun," *New Scientist*, October 19, 2006, www.newscientist.com/article/dn10336-gold-mine-holds-life-untouched-by-the-sun.html (accessed January 23, 2010).

p. 27, "In the inky darkness around these vents . . .": "The Legendary Ocean—The Unexplored Frontier," National Oceanic and Atmospheric Administration, 1998, www .yoto98.noaa.gov/yoto/meeting/mar_expl_316.html (accessed February 2, 2010).

p. 28, "New Yorkers identified 479 species . . .": "Central Park BioBlitz 2006." The Explorers Club, n.d., www.explorers .org/projects/bioblitz/bioblitz2006/bioblitz2006.php (accessed February 17, 2010).

p. 28, "The 2007 BioBlitz, held in Washington, DC's . . .": "BioBlitz 2007: Washington, DC's Rock Creek Park." National Geographic Society, 2009, www .nationalgeographic.com/field/projects/bioblitz-dc-2007.html (accessed February 17, 2010).

p. 28, "Surveyors for the 2008 BioBlitz in North Shore . . .": "BioBlitz Aukland 2008," Landcare Research, 2010, www.landcareresearch.co.nz/research/biosystematics/ bioblitz/auckland2008/index.asp (accessed February 17, 2010).

p. 30, "Virunga is Africa's oldest national park . . .": David Braun, "Rangers Rout Illegal Charcoal Operations in Africa's Gorilla Park," August 3, 2009, http://blogs.nationalgeographic.com/blogs/news/ chiefeditor/2009/08/rangers-rout-virunga-charcoal-operators.html (accessed April 30, 2010).

p. 30, ". . . nearly $160 billion per year changes hands . . .": Millennium Ecosystem Assessment Board, p. 98.

p. 30, ". . . about 28 percent of the world's fish stocks . . .": Food and Agriculture Organization of the United Nations, "Chapter 3: World Review of Fisheries and Aquaculture," in The State of World Fisheries and Aquaculture 2008 (Rome: UN Food and Agriculture

Organization, 2009), www.fao.org/docrep/011/i0250e/
i0250e00.htm (accessed February 27, 2010), pp. 6–7.

p. 30, ". . . between 2000 and 2005, an average of 18 million
acres . . .": Food and Agriculture Organization of the
United Nations, "15 Key Findings," *Global Forest
Resources Assessment 2005* (Rome: 2006), www.fao.org/
forestry/fra/fra2005/en/ (accessed February 12, 2010).

p. 31, ". . . forests hold 50 percent more carbon dioxide . . ." :
Food and Agriculture Organization of the United
Nations (2006).

p. 32, ". . . Brazil has 7,780 species of trees.": Food and
Agriculture Organization of the United Nations (2006).

Chapter Three
p. 33, "In March 2010 almost 309 million people . . .": "U.S.
& World Population Clocks," U.S. Census Bureau,
December 2009, www.census.gov/main/www/
popclock.html (accessed March 19, 2010).

p. 33, "The 534 residents of Achille, Oklahoma . . .": "Achille,
Oklahoma," City Data, 2010, www.city-data.com/city/
Achille-Oklahoma.html (accessed March 2, 2010).

p. 34, "A total of fourteen terrestrial . . .": "Major Habitat
Types," World Wildlife Fund, n.d., www.panda.org/
about_our_earth/ecoregions/about/habitat_types/
(accessed January 30, 2010).

p. 34, "Ecologist Barry Commoner once described . . .":
Barry Commoner, *The Closing Circle: Nature, Man &
Technology* (New York: Knopf, 1971), p. 14.

p. 40, "I have watched the face of many a newly wolfless . . ."
Aldo Leopold, *A Sand County Almanac* (New York:
Ballantine Books, 1966), pp. 139–140.

p. 40, "The most common is nitrogen . . .": Clive Dobson and Gregor Gilpin Beck, Watersheds: A Practical Handbook for Healthy Water (Toronto: Firefly Books, 1999), p. 31.

p. 41, "On average, 60 percent of human body weight . . .": David Suzuki with Amanda McConnell, *The Sacred Balance: Rediscovering Our Place in Nature* (Amherst, NY: Prometheus Books, 1997), p. 59.

p. 42, ". . . more than 100 pounds (45 kilograms) per week . . .": Barbara Mayer, "Marine Debris: Cigarette Lighters and Plastic Problem on Midway Atoll," U.S. Fish and Wildlife Service, Summer 2003, www.fws.gov/midway/ Midway_Atoll_NWR_Cigarette_Lighters.pdf (accessed May 6, 2010).

p. 42, "Located approximately 1,250 miles . . .": Midway Atoll National Wildlife Refuge, "About Us," U.S. Fish and Wildlife Service, March 22, 2010, www.fws.gov/ midway/aboutus.html (accessed May 6, 2010).

p. 42, "In 2004 biologists found a dead albatross . . .": Kenneth R. Weiss, "Plague of Plastic Chokes the Sea," *Los Angeles Times*, August 2, 2006, www.latimes.com/ news/printedition/la-me-ocean2aug02,0,5594900 .story?page = 1 (accessed May 2, 2010).

p. 43, "Volunteers who clean up trash at Midway Atoll . . .": Barbara Mayer (2003).

p. 45, ". . . archaean ecosystems approximately 3.5 billion years ago.": Groombridge and Jenkins, p. 24.

Chapter Four

p. 46, ". . . reaching a speed of 200 miles per hour . . .": "Peregrine Falcon," National Geographic Society, 2010, http://animals.nationalgeographic.com/animals/birds/ peregrine-falcon/ (accessed March 22, 2010).

p. 47, ". . . eat 90 percent of monarch caterpillars.": "Monarch Butterfly," Journey North, 2003, www.learner.org/jnorth/ tm/monarch/ExpertAnswer03.html (accessed February 18, 2010).

p. 52, "Researchers found that young salmon infected . . .": Robin Meadows, "Salmon Farms Create Deadly Clouds of Sea Lice," *Conservation*, January–March 2007, www .conservationmagazine.org/articles/v8n1/salmon-farms-create-deadly-clouds-of-sea-lice/ (accessed April 30, 2010).

p. 53, "At least a hundred migratory bird species . . .": Laura Tangley, "Taking Birding to New Heights," *National Wildlife*, June/July 2008, pp. 42–43.

p. 53, "Ecologist Robert DeCandido, who organizes surveys . . ." Robert DeCandido, "Dancing in the Moonlight: Nocturnal Bird Migration from the Top of the Empire State Building," *Winging It*, May/June 2004, pp. 3–5.

p. 54, "According to the U.S. Fish and Wildlife Service . . .": U.S. Fish and Wildlife Service, "Important Facts about Habitat Loss and Birds," May 1999, http://library.fws .gov/pubs/mbd_habitat_loss.pdf (accessed April 28, 2010).

p. 56, "The godwits spend a couple of weeks eating extra portions . . .": Eric Wagner, "Solving the Mystery of a Migratory Marvel," *National Wildlife*, December/ January 2008, pp. 18–20.

p. 56, "Hibernating bats can survive temperatures . . .": J. R. Speakman and D. R. Thomas, "Physiological ecology and energetics of bats," in eds. T. H. Kunz and M. B. Fenton, *Bat Ecology* (Chicago: University of Chicago Press, 2003), p. 459.

p. 56, "Under normal circumstances it takes a bat . . .":

Gerhard Neuweiler, *The Biology of Bats* (New York: Oxford University Press, 2000), pp. 76–80.

p. 58, "A single disturbance may use . . .": Speakman and Thomas, p. 462.

p. 60, ". . . global temperatures have increased 0.7 to 1.4°F . . .": NASA, "Global Warming," n.d., www.nasa.gov/worldbook/global_warming_worldbook.html (accessed March 23, 2010).

p. 60, "A 2006 study of more than 560 European . . .": Annette Menzel, "European Phenological Response to Climate Change Matches the Warming Pattern," *Global Change Biology*, 2006, www.creaf.uab.es/ecophysiology/pdfs%20grup/pdfs/menzel%20etalGCB2006.pdf (accessed May 1, 2010).

Chapter Five

p. 61, "In the mid–1600s, when Steno was born . . .": "Nicholas Steno (1638–1686)," University of California Museum of Paleontology Web, 2000, www.ucmp.berkeley.edu/history/steno.html (accessed July 27, 2009).

p. 62, "On the basis of the amount of erosion . . .": "Uniformitarianism: Charles Lyell," University of California Museum of Paleontology Web, 2006, http://evolution.berkeley.edu/evosite/history/uniformitar.shtml (accessed February 18, 2010).

p. 62, "In 1815 William Smith used Steno's geological . . .": "William Smith," University of California Museum of Paleontology Web, 1996, www.ucmp.berkeley.edu/history/smith.html (accessed February 18, 2010).

p. 63, "Darwin saw evidence from around the world . . .": Charles Darwin, *The Voyage of the Beagle* (Hertfordshire, UK: Wordsworth Editions, 1997 [1890]), p. 306.

p. 64, "When the *Beagle* stopped at Punta Alta, Argentina . . .": Darwin, *The Voyage of the Beagle*, pp. 79–80.

p. 64. ". . . the naturalist in travelling, for instance . . .": Charles Darwin, *The Origin of Species* (New York: Barnes & Noble, 2004 [1859]), p. 279.

p. 65, ". . . seeing this gradation and diversity of structure . . .": Darwin, *The Voyage of the Beagle*, p. 361.

p. 66, "In 1858 they agreed to make a presentation . . .": "The Darwin and Wallace Joint Paper," Natural History Museum, www.nhm.ac.uk/nature-online/collections-at-the-museum/ (accessed August 16, 2009).

p. 66, "In 1933 the U.S. National Park Service set aside . . .": William Conrod, "A Desert Galápagos," *Natural History*, May 2008, pp. 16–18.

p. 68, "A single dune may move as much as 30 feet . . .": "White Sands National Monument," U.S. National Park Service, March 20, 2010, www.nps.gov/whsa/index.htm (accessed March 22, 2010)

p. 68, "Whiptail lizards are usually boldly colorful . . .": Conrod, p. 17.

p. 68, "Deer mice have also changed color at White Sands.": "Color Genes Help Mice and Lizards," *Science*, July 15, 2005, www.nps.gov/whsa/naturescience/upload/Rosenblum_SciencePress.pdf (accessed March 3, 2010).

p. 70, "A study conducted at New Mexico State University . . .": Conrod, p. 17.

p. 71, "With an altitude of 9,677 feet . . .": "Mount St. Helens Volcano, Washington," U.S. Geological Survey, October 7, 2008, http://vulcan.wr.usgs.gov/Volcanoes/MSH/description_msh.html (accessed January 18, 2010).

p. 71, "At 8:32 a.m., Mount St. Helens shuddered . . .": "May 18, 1980 Eruption of Mount St. Helens," U.S. Geological Survey, March 28, 2005, http://vulcan.wr.usgs.gov/Volcanoes/MSH/May18/description_may18_1980.html (accessed January 18, 2010).

p. 71, ". . . at speeds up to 680 miles per hour . . .": U.S. Geological Survey (March 28, 2005).

p. 72, "The first known mass extinction . . .": Groombridge and Jenkins, p. 30.

p. 74, "When ecologists examined the most damaged sites . . .": Virginia H. Dale et al., "Plant Succession on the Mount St. Helens Debris-Avalanche Deposit," U.S. Forest Service, 2005, www.treesearch.fs.fed.us/pubs/25524 (accessed February 2, 2010).

p. 74, "In the 1850s ranchers decided that Santa Cruz . . .": Jason Van Driesche and Roy Van Driesche, "After the Sheep Are Gone," *Conservation*, Fall 2001, www.conservationmagazine.org/articles/v2n4/after-the-sheep-are-gone/ (accessed April 28, 2010).

Chapter Six

p. 77, "In plants and irrational animals, the view . . .": Thomas Malthus, *An Essay on the Principle of Population* (1826), Library of Economics and Liberty, 2000, www.econlib.org/library/Malthus/malPlong1.html#Chapter % 20I (accessed March 2, 2010), paragraph I.I.6.

p. 78, "In the northern states of America . . . .": Malthus, paragraph I.I.11.

p. 78, "Approximately one hundred men established the first . . .": Faith Jaycox, *The Colonial Era*, (New York: Facts on File, 2002), p. 75.

p. 78, "By 1775, just before the American Revolution . . .": Edwin J. Perkins, *The Economy of Colonial America* (New York: Columbia University Press, 1988), p. 2.

p. 78, ". . . black walnuts and related trees produce a toxic . . .": "Black Walnut," U.S. Forest Service, November 1993, http://hort.ufl.edu/trees/JUGNIGA.pdf (accessed March 12, 2010).

p. 79, "Researchers once caught a blue jay . . .": "Blue Jay," Cornell Lab of Ornithology's All about Birds, 2009, www.allaboutbirds.org/guide/Blue_Jay/lifehistory (accessed March 7, 2010).

p. 81, "In the winter of 2004–05, more than . . .": Frances Backhouse, "Ghost Chasers," *Audubon Magazine*, n.d., www.audubonmagazine.org/birds/birds1001.html (accessed January 17, 2010).

p. 82, "How do these birds avoid competition?": Chris C. Fisher and Joseph Morlan, *Birds of San Francisco and the Bay Area* (Redmond, WA: Lone Pine, 1996), pp. 54–67.

p. 83, "The Russian ecologist Georgii Gause . . .": Carl Hoagstrom, "Competitive Exclusion Principle," Encyclopedia of Earth, www.eoearth.org/article/Competitive_exclusion_principle (accessed February 9, 2010).

p. 85, ". . . of 47,677 well-studied species worldwide . . .": John Platt, "IUCN Red List Update," *Scientific American*, November 2, 2009, www.scientificamerican.com/blog/post.cfm?id = iucn-red-list-update-17291-species-2009-11-02 (accessed March 3, 2010).

p. 86, "We abuse the land because we regard it . . .": Aldo Leopold, pp. xviii–xix.

p. 86, "Two decades later, Senator Gaylord Nelson . . .": Gaylord Nelson, "How the First Earth Day Came

About," EnviroLink, n.d., http://earthday.envirolink
.org/history.html (accessed March 21, 2010).

p. 86, "So long as the human species inhabits the Earth . . .":
Gaylord Nelson, "Earth Day '70: What It Meant,"
U.S. Environmental Protection Agency, August 12,
2009, www.epa.gov/history/topics/earthday/02.htm
(accessed March 24, 2010).

Further Information

Books

Desonie, Dana. *Biosphere: Ecosystems and Biodiversity Loss.* New York: Chelsea House, 2007.

Eldredge, Niles, and Susan Pearson. *Charles Darwin and the Mystery of Mysteries.* New York: Flash Point, 2010.

Gerdes, Louise, ed. *Biodiversity.* Detroit: Greenhaven Press, 2010.

Silverstein, Alvin, Virginia Silverstein, and Laura Silverstein Nunno. *Photosynthesis.* Minneapolis: Twenty-first Century Books, 2008.

Simpson, Kathleen. *Genetics: From DNA to Designer Dogs.* Washington, DC: National Geographic Society, 2008.

DVDs

Arthus-Bertrand, Yann (Dir.). *Home.* Twentieth Century Fox, 2009.

Attenborough, David. *Life.* BBC Warner, 2010.

National Geographic. *Human Footprint.* National Geographic, 2008.

Websites

Biomes of the World
www.mbgnet.net
The Missouri Botanical Garden offers a close-up look at each of Earth's major biomes.

Conservation International
www.conservation.org
This organization works with cultures around the world to conserve natural systems and protect resources that benefit us all.

The Diversity of Life
www.mnh.si.edu/explore/diversity.htm
Hosted by the Smithsonian Institution's National Museum of Natural History, this site offers articles describing aspects of Earth's biodiversity.

Encyclopedia of Earth
www.eoearth.org
Scholars and experts from around the world have compiled the information in this online reference. Users can research topics related to Earth's physical environment and natural systems and their impact on human beings.

High School Environmental Center
www.epa.gov/highschool
These resources, collected by the U.S. Environmental Protection Agency, cover topics from ecosystems to recycling and health.

Prehistoric Time Line
http://science.nationalgeographic.com/science/prehistoric-world/prehistoric-time-line.html
National Geographic has compiled an interactive time line featuring details about important events in Earth's history, from the formation of the first rocks to the appearance of early humans.

Understanding Evolution
http://evolution.berkeley.edu
The University of California at Berkeley offers this review of the major mechanisms of and evidence for evolution.

Young Naturalist Awards
www.amnh.org/nationalcenter/youngnaturalistawards
Interested in conducting your own investigation of the living world? The American Museum of Natural History offers an annual science competition for students in grades 7 through 12.

Bibliography

Brown, Joseph E. *The Return of the Brown Pelican*. Baton Rouge: Louisiana State University Press, 1983.

Commoner, Barry. *The Closing Circle: Nature, Man and Technology*. New York: Knopf, 1971.

Darwin, Charles. *The Origin of Species* (1859). New York: Barnes & Noble, 2004.

———. *The Voyage of the* Beagle (1890). Hertfordshire, UK: Wordsworth Editions, 1997.

Dobson, Clive, and Gregor Gilpin Beck. *Watersheds: A Practical Handbook for Healthy Water*. Toronto: Firefly Books, 1999.

Fisher, Chris C., and Joseph Morlan, *Birds of San Francisco and the Bay Area*. Redmond, WA: Lone Pine, 1996.

Food and Agriculture Organization of the United Nations. *Global Forest Resources Assessment 2005*. Rome: FAO, 2006, www.fao. org/forestry/fra/fra2005/en/ (accessed February 12, 2010).

———. *State of World Fisheries and Aquaculture 2008*. Rome: FAO, 2009.

Groombridge, Brian, and Martin D. Jenkins. *World Atlas of Biodiversity.* Berkeley: University of California Press, 2002.

Hails, Chris, ed. *Living Planet Report 2008.* Gland, Switzerland: WWF International, 2008.

Jaycox, Faith. *The Colonial Era.* New York: Facts on File, 2002.

Kunz, T. H., and M. B. Fenton, eds., *Bat Ecology.* Chicago: University of Chicago Press, 2003.

Leopold, Aldo. *Round River.* New York: Oxford University Press, 1993.

———. *A Sand County Almanac.* New York: Ballantine Books, 1966.

Malthus, Thomas. *An Essay on the Principle of Population* (1826). New York: Dover, 2007.

Millennium Ecosystem Assessment Board. *Ecosystems and Human Well-Being: Biodiversity Synthesis.* Washington, DC: Island Press, 2005, www.maweb.org/en/index.aspx (accessed January 23, 2010).

———. *Ecosystems and Human Well-Being: Current State and Trends.* Washington, DC: Island Press, 2005, www.maweb. org/en/index.aspx (accessed January 23, 2010).

Muir, John. *My First Summer in the Sierra.* In *Nature Writings.* New York: Library of America, 1992.

Neuweiler, Gerhard. *The Biology of Bats.* New York: Oxford University Press, 2000.

Perkins, Edwin J. *The Economy of Colonial America.* New York: Columbia University Press, 1988.

Suzuki, David, with Amanda McConnell. *The Sacred Balance: Rediscovering Our Place in Nature.* Amherst, NY: Prometheus Books, 1997.

Tattersall, I., and J. H. Schwartz. *Extinct Humans.* New York: Westview Press, 2000.

Index

Pages in **boldface** are illustrations.

About the Author

Christine Petersen has enjoyed diverse careers as a bat biologist and a middle school teacher. Now a freelance writer, she has published more than forty nonfiction books for children and young adults. When she is not writing, Petersen conducts naturalist programs near her Minnesota home and spends time with her young son. Petersen's work has been recognized by the American Association for the Advancement of Science (AAAS), and she is a member of the Society of Children's Book Writers and Illustrators.